PARENTAL ALIENATION

Understanding, Recognizing, Intervening

Mariangela Campus

First English-language edition: 2026

ISBN (paperback): [to be assigned]

Published by Marix Institute Rome–New York

Disclaimer

This book is intended exclusively for informational and educational purposes. The analyses, reflections, and descriptions it contains refer to relational dynamics of a general nature and are not attributable to real persons, to specific cases, or to any particular legal proceeding.

This work does not constitute psychological, psychotherapeutic, medical, legal, or forensic advice, nor does it replace, in any way, individualized professional assessment. Every concrete situation requires specific evaluation by licensed professionals under the applicable laws of the relevant jurisdiction.

Any descriptions of personality traits, psychodynamic configurations, or behavioral patterns are not intended to formulate diagnoses or to attach clinical labels to particular individuals. Every reference to psychological categories or theoretical constructs is to be understood in a descriptive and phenomenological sense, not a diagnostic one.

This book analyzes observable conduct, not personal identities. No page of this text should be read as an accusation, a moral judgment, or an attribution of blame to any category of persons.

The author declines all responsibility for any improper, decontextualized, or instrumental use of the contents of this work, including its use in legal proceedings without adequate specialized professional assessment.

The reader bears full responsibility for the use made of the information contained in this book.

A Note on Language

The terms "alienating parent" and "targeted parent" are used in a functional and descriptive sense, to indicate a role within a relational dynamic — not an identity. Likewise, the expression "alienated child" describes an adaptive condition, not a personality trait and not a fault. The language of this book favors communicative clarity while respecting clinical complexity.

To every child who was robbed of the right to love freely.
To every parent who searched for the words and could not find them.

To you,
parents and grandparents,
who have known the pain of being shut out
of the life of someone you love.
To you who waited for a phone call
that never came.
A message. A sign.
To you who learned what it means
to feel the presence of a child or a grandchild
even when the house has gone silent.
No one prepared you
for an absence without explanation.
For a rejection that does not resemble the heart
you raised.
You went on loving
without being able to show it.
You guarded memories
the way one guards something fragile and alive.
You resisted the temptation
to turn pain into resentment.
This book is for you.
To tell you that your love
was not wasted.
That your presence
has left traces.
Because true love
cannot be erased by a story.
It does not go out with silence.
It cannot be rewritten by fear.
It remains. And it waits.
Mariangela Campus

A Note on Method

This book was not born as an academic treatise or a clinical manual. It grew out of the author's personal experience as a mother caught in a situation of parental alienation, and out of years of listening and dialogue carried on through a national association that gathers the testimony of parents and family members affected by the same phenomenon. The reflections in this volume weave those experiences together with the international scientific literature on parental alienation, in order to offer the reader an accessible, well-informed key to a phenomenon that, when it goes unnamed, continues to operate undisturbed. The sources were selected with a preference for cornerstone studies, citable in forensic evaluation and in court: Baker's work on the long-term effects of alienation in adult children, Warshak's on parental programming, Bernet's on nosographic classification, Harman, Kruk, and Hines's on alienating behaviors as a form of family violence, Ceci and Bruck's on the suggestibility of children's testimony, Garber's on dynamic rather than diagnostic reading, Bowlby's on attachment theory, and Siegel's on the neurobiology of development. The twenty relational dynamics described in Part I are the author's original framework, developed by integrating the international scientific contributions with direct observation gathered through years of advocacy work and with the lived experience of parents, children, and family members involved in situations of parental alienation. They are not a reproduction or direct adaptation of pre-existing theoretical models. The categories used in this book do not represent individual clinical diagnoses, nor are they meant to attach pathological labels to particular persons. References to personality traits, defensive configurations, or relational patterns have descriptive and phenomenological value. Every family situation requires specific, multidisciplinary, contextualized assessment. The testimonies reported in this text come from direct interviews conducted over the years with children — now adults — who grew up inside contexts of parental alienation. Names have been omitted, identifying details altered, and the narratives reorganized without distorting their deeper meaning.

This book is no substitute for clinical, psychotherapeutic, or legal consultation. Its purposes are informational, educational, and awareness-raising. It is intended for parents, family members, professionals, and anyone who wishes to understand the phenomenon with rigor and without oversimplification.

CONTENTS

PART I — UNDERSTANDING PARENTAL ALIENATION

1. Why This Book

This book was born of a precise necessity: to bring clarity to a field dominated by confusion, ideological shortcuts, and narratives that obscure what ought to remain central — the protection of the child.

Those who come to these pages, in most cases, do not come out of theoretical curiosity. They arrive after months or years of bewilderment, pain, disbelief. They arrive because something has broken in the relationship with their child, and no explanation they have received so far has managed to make sense of what is happening.

Parental alienation is a complex phenomenon. It involves emotional bonds, deep feelings, family roles, dynamics of power and, in many cases, the court system. To reduce all of this to a slogan, or to a contest between "good" parents and "bad" ones, is to fail the very people who suffer its deepest and most lasting consequences. Nor is it a marginal phenomenon: according to prevalence surveys of representative United States samples (Harman, Leder-Elder & Biringen, 2019), alienating behaviors affect roughly 22 million parents in the United States alone — a figure that conveys the epidemiological scale of a problem too often treated as an exception.

This book was not written to take sides against mothers or against fathers. It was written to understand a process that develops over time, often silently, and that can profoundly alter the bond between a child and one of their parents. To understand is not to justify. It is to look reality in the face, even when reality is uncomfortable or destabilizing.

A child is not an ally, a judge, or an emotional mediator. A child is a person in formation, who builds identity, a sense of safety, and the capacity for relationships through the bond with both parents. When one of those bonds is systematically devalued, denied, or destroyed, the damage reaches the child's entire emotional architecture: the way they will learn to love, to trust, to perceive themselves and others. Baker (2007) documented that adults who were exposed to alienating behaviors in childhood report, with very high frequency, depression, low self-esteem, and significant difficulties in intimate relationships: the full data will be presented in Chapter 11.

The book is meant for parents who have been shut out of their children's lives or progressively pushed to the margins; for grandparents and relatives who watch, powerless, as a bond is severed; for people caught in high-conflict separations; and for professionals who want to understand the phenomenon with rigor and without impenetrable jargon.

In Brief. Parental alienation is a relational process that develops over time, not a slogan for taking sides. This book exists to give words and criteria to those who live it and to those who must assess it, keeping one thing at the center: the protection of the child. To understand is not to justify: it is to look reality in the face.

2. Definition and Recognition

Before turning to the definition, one premise is essential. Not every refusal is alienation. A child may reject a parent for reasons that deserve to be heard and protected — not corrected.

The child may have suffered physical, psychological, or sexual abuse. They may have witnessed the mistreatment of the parent they live with. They may have endured serious neglect, exposure to dangerous conduct, or the chronic emotional instability of the adult. In these cases the refusal is not pathological: it is protective. And it is the child's right.

There are at least five situations in which a child's rejection of a parent should not be attributed to alienation. Reactive refusal, which follows inappropriate parental behavior that the child has experienced directly. Physiological conflict, which appears in many separations without any active conditioning. Adolescent refusal, tied to the developmental processes of individuation typical of that age. Post-traumatic refusal, the consequence of direct experiences of violence or abuse. And detachment from an inadequate parent — one who may struggle with addiction, instability, or an incapacity to provide care.

Parental alienation is a dysfunctional family dynamic in which a child rejects an adequate, affectionately available parent as a result of psychological manipulation exerted by the other parent. It arises chiefly in the context of separation and divorce.

The Five Most Frequent Diagnostic Errors

The improper application of the concept of parental alienation generates clinical and judicial errors with grave consequences. It is worth describing the most frequent.

The first is the confusion between refusal and alienation. A child may reject a parent for reasons that have nothing to do with conditioning: well-founded fear, direct traumatic experience, parental inadequacy as the child perceives it, an ordinary loyalty conflict that no one induced. Refusal, in itself, is not an indicator of alienation. It becomes one only when an active, sustained process of conditioning by the other parent can be documented, in the absence of autonomous causes within the child (Garber, 2020).

The second error is what Johnston (2003) called "alignment": the child sides with one parent not because they have been manipulated, but because they perceive — correctly or not — that parent as more vulnerable, more in need of protection, or simply more present. Alignment is an adaptive response to conflict, not the product of a strategy. To treat it as alienation is to pathologize a survival mechanism.

The third error is causal inversion: attributing the refusal to conditioning when the refusal predates the separation. If a child was already showing distress in the relationship with a parent before the marital crisis, any later conditioning — even where present — is not the primary cause of the refusal. Chronology matters.

The fourth is the gender error. International research documents that alienating behaviors can be enacted by mothers and fathers alike (Harman, Kruk & Hines, 2018), and that representative samples show no statistically significant gender differences (Harman et al., 2023). In courtroom practice, however, the accusation of alienation is leveled more often against mothers, and more often in response to allegations of domestic violence (Meier, 2020). This fact imposes an additional caution: every assessment must rule out the possibility that an alienation claim is being used as a defensive tool to delegitimize a well-founded report of abuse.

The fifth is what we might call the instrument error: using the concept of alienation as a binary category — present or absent — instead of as a continuum. In many separated, high-conflict families, elements of conditioning coexist with legitimate reasons for refusal, with inadequacies on both sides, with alignment no one induced. To flatten this complexity into a label — "there is alienation" or "there is no alienation" — is an epistemological error before it is a clinical one. As Fidler and Bala (2010) observe, post-separation contact refusal is a multifactorial phenomenon that demands individualized, multidimensional assessment.

The Burden of Proof in Clinical Evaluation

Whoever hypothesizes the presence of parental alienation bears the burden of documenting it through converging indicators: observable, repeated alienating behaviors in the suspected parent; a temporal progression of the refusal that correlates with those behaviors; the absence of autonomous causes within the child; and consistency with the patterns described in the literature. Absent that converging documentation, the hypothesis of alienation remains a hypothesis —

and treating it as a certainty exposes the child to the risk of being separated from a protective parent.

This chapter exists because the risk of error runs in both directions: failing to recognize real alienation is as grave as diagnosing an alienation that does not exist. Both errors inflict deep and often irreversible damage on the child.

This book contains no moral verdicts, no automatic assignments of blame, no miracle solutions. It contains words for naming what is happening, intelligible keys for reading it, and a frame that restores meaning and dignity to the experience.

In Brief. Not every refusal is alienation: there are protective, reactive, and developmentally ordinary refusals. We speak of alienation only when a child rejects an adequate parent because of the other parent's documentable manipulation. The five diagnostic errors and the burden of proof cut in both directions: failing to recognize real alienation is as serious as diagnosing one that does not exist.

3. Why a Child Can Be Manipulated

When we speak of manipulating a minor, a basic error is often made: the child or adolescent is imagined as a "smaller version" of the adult, equipped with the same inner tools, the same capacity for choice, the same emotional freedom. A minor does not yet possess a complete psychological and neural architecture.

This is not a judgment: it is a fact. Understanding how the brain grows, how critical thinking develops, and how identity is built is essential to understanding why instilling rigid, distorted, or false convictions in a child is not merely possible but often relatively easy. The major theories of child development confirm that critical thinking and identity formation consolidate only gradually. Jean Piaget's studies (1970) showed that formal logical thought emerges fully only in adolescence, while Erik Erikson (1968) demonstrated that the formation of personal identity passes through delicate developmental stages, profoundly shaped by primary attachment figures. Contemporary neuroscience further confirms that the prefrontal cortex — the region responsible for critical scrutiny, the weighing of information, and emotional regulation — completes its maturation only in early adulthood. Within this developmental picture, the systematic induction of rigid or distorted convictions is not only possible: it is made easier by the child's natural emotional dependence on the significant adult. A child does not think in order to be free. A child thinks in order to feel safe.

Conviction as Protection

Many convictions, especially in children, are not born to describe reality as completely as possible. They are born to protect: from pain, from the fear of losing someone, from feeling torn in two.

When a child says with absolute certainty "I don't want to see my father anymore" or "I don't want to see my mother anymore," they are not necessarily expressing a free and considered choice. Often they are expressing the way they have found to stop hurting. That conviction erases longing, extinguishes guilt, closes the loyalty conflict. It works like an emotional shield: it is not a conscious lie, and it is not calculated manipulation. It is an adaptation. If one tries to "correct" the conviction without understanding what it protects against, one risks stripping away the only equilibrium the child has found. This explains why many such convictions are so rigid and so resistant to challenge: questioning them would mean feeling worse, not better.

Conviction and freedom are not the same thing. A widespread misunderstanding holds that feeling certain means being free. The truth is usually the opposite. Psychological freedom is not recognized by the absence of doubt but by the capacity to tolerate ambivalence, to change one's mind, to ask questions without feeling that doing so endangers one's identity or one's bonds. When a conviction admits no nuance, tolerates no questions, and is experienced as "non-negotiable," we are not looking at a free choice but at an emotional necessity. The more rigid a conviction, the less room it leaves for inner freedom. In the alienated child the conviction serves a precise function: holding together what would otherwise collapse. When an adult challenges it head-on, the result is usually the opposite of the one intended: the child stiffens, closes up, defends the position more fiercely.

Persuasion, Influence, and Manipulation: A Necessary Distinction

Not every influence is manipulation. Persuasion exists only where a person can weigh alternatives, dissent, and change their mind without losing an important emotional bond.

Influence is a normal phenomenon: parents influence children, teachers influence students, cultural models influence individuals. It is healthy when it is plural, reversible, non-exclusive. Manipulation is different. It works on fear, not on reason. It conditions love, not opinion. It narrows alternatives instead of widening them. Dissent carries an emotional price: doubting is dangerous, changing one's mind amounts to betrayal. The subject complies not out of conviction but because they cannot afford not to.

If an adult can be manipulated, how easily can a child be? The belief that adults are "immune" to manipulation is a comforting fantasy — and a false one. History, social psychology, and clinical practice show that educated, apparently autonomous adults can be profoundly manipulated.

Abusive Relationships

In many relationships, adult women come to justify violent behavior, to internalize guilt that is not theirs, to defend the very person who harms them. The mechanisms are well known and well documented: progressive isolation, as the victim is cut off from her social network until she is alone with the manipulator; intermittent reinforcement, moments of tenderness alternating with violence in a paradoxical bond; induced guilt, as the victim is brought to believe that every conflict is her fault; systematic devaluation, as self-esteem is eroded day after day. These women are neither stupid nor complicit. They are people whose need for attachment has been intercepted and weaponized. Many describe, in hindsight, the same experience: "I knew something was wrong. But I couldn't trust what I was feeling." That mechanism — losing faith in one's own perception — reappears in parental alienation: the child, like the abused partner, stops trusting what they feel, because they have learned that feeling is dangerous. Often these same women — victims of psychological, economic, or coercive abuse — find, once they become aware of the violence and pull away from it, that the conflict assumes a new form: the manipulative partner, having lost control over the woman, transfers the battle to the parental plane, adopting alienating conduct aimed at striking the mother through her bond with the children. In these cases separation does not interrupt the dynamic of domination; it reorganizes it, shifting the axis of manipulation from the couple to the parent-child relationship.

Cult Dynamics

Cult dynamics are an even more extreme example. Adults — often cultured, high-functioning people — come to renounce critical thinking, hand over resources and autonomy, accept irrational narratives, and sever ties with anyone who questions the group. The leader does not say: "Give up your freedom." The leader says: "I understand you as no one else does." Doubt is not forbidden; it is made emotionally unbearable.

Those who leave cults often say the same thing: "It's not that I didn't see the contradictions. It's that I couldn't afford to see them." That sentence could be spoken, word for word, by an alienated child grown to adulthood.

Propaganda and Groupthink

No individual relationship is required for manipulation to work. When a piece of information is repeated often enough, by sources perceived as authoritative, in a context where dissent is discouraged, most adults end up absorbing it as true.

Solomon Asch demonstrated this in the 1950s: educated adults, faced with a unanimous group, went so far as to deny the evidence of their own eyes. Seventy-five percent of subjects conformed at least once to the group's plainly wrong judgment (Asch, 1956). Stanley Milgram went further: sixty-five percent of participants agreed to deliver what they believed was a maximum-voltage electric shock to a stranger, at the direction of an authority figure (Milgram, 1963). If adults in full cognitive maturity yield to social pressure and authority in artificial, temporary settings, it is reasonable to ask: what happens to a child — whose prefrontal cortex has not finished maturing, whose critical thinking is still under construction, whose very survival depends entirely on the adult caring for them — when the pressure is not that of a laboratory experiment but the daily, constant pressure of the parent they live with?

The answer comes from research on children's suggestibility. Ceci and Bruck (1995), in their systematic work on children's testimony, demonstrated that children — above all in preschool and early school years — are significantly more vulnerable than adults to suggestive questions, to the repetition of false information, and to the influence of authority figures. Children can incorporate into their own memory events they never lived, if those events are recounted often enough, and with enough conviction, by a trusted adult. This is not deliberate lying: it is memory reconstruction, a process in which the original memory is progressively replaced or contaminated by the repeated narrative. This finding is central to understanding the alienating dynamic. The alienating parent does not ask the child to lie. In the great majority of cases, the parent builds a narrative context in which the child comes to believe — authentically — that the rejected parent is dangerous, inadequate, or indifferent. The child is not playing a part: the child is living a reconstructed reality. That is why the refusal looks so convincing, and why it is so hard to take apart.

The Structural Vulnerability of the Child

A child's brain is built around one fundamental priority: surviving through relationship. The emotional regions develop before the critical ones. The implicit question is not "is this true?" but "am I safe?"

The prefrontal cortex — responsible for critical thinking, the integration of information, and autonomous decision-making — completes its maturation between the ages of twenty and twenty-five (Siegel, 2020). This means a child lacks the equipment to distinguish reliably among reality, interpretation, and suggestion. As Ceci and Bruck (1995) documented, a child's suggestibility is at its highest when the source of the information is an attachment figure: the child tends to absorb the adult's narrative as their own, above all when it eases their anxiety.

That vulnerability is not uniform: it depends on when, in the course of development, the relational pressure strikes. Perry's neurosequential model

(Perry & Szalavitz, 2017) shows that the brain matures from the bottom up — from the brainstem regions that regulate stress to the cortical regions of critical thought. Early relational experiences, repeated and charged with tension, imprint themselves first on the lower systems, the systems of survival, and only later become accessible to reasoning. This is why the age at which the alienating dynamic begins is not a biographical detail: it determines how deeply the induced narrative takes root. The earlier the exposure, the more the rupture of the bond is encoded as a bodily datum before it ever becomes an idea — and the harder it will be, later, to reach it with words alone.

During adolescence, thought becomes more articulate, but the vulnerability remains. An adolescent talks like an adult: argues, defends positions, appears certain. It is precisely that certainty which misleads the outside observer. Neurobiologically, however, the emotional and motivational systems are running at full throttle while the prefrontal cortex is still maturing. If a narrative reduces anxiety, supplies an identity, and protects a bond perceived as vital, an adolescent can embrace it with absolute conviction — not because they are free, but because it stabilizes them.

Chronological Age Is Not Psychological Autonomy

Adult systems are not immune either. There is a truth that is hard to accept when speaking of parental alienation: adult institutions are not immune to the seduction of narrative coherence.

Schools, courts, child-welfare and health services often operate under pressure: heavy caseloads, scarce time, enormous responsibility, fear of error. In that context, emotional complexity becomes an operational problem. Certainty, by contrast, becomes a solution.

A child who speaks coherently, who appears convinced, who shows no ambivalence, hands the system a closed account. It requires no further steps, opens no contradictions, demands no multi-level reading. Systems, in order to function, tend to prefer what is "legible." Mistaking coherence for credibility is the most frequent cognitive error in the assessment of alienation cases: narrative coherence — the reader will meet this idea again throughout the book — is often evidence of adaptation, not of truth.

When systems listen to the content without interrogating the process, when they isolate the account from its relational context, they treat a narrative as a recording of facts rather than as a construction. The result is assessments that are formally correct and psychologically blind. The school that says "we don't get involved in family matters" is taking a side, even when it does not know it. To accept without question the child's version, a parent's absence, the prevailing story, is to ratify a dynamic already underway. The court, for its part, tends to treat the child's stated will as an expression of autonomy and an index of truth. But if no distinction is drawn between subjective conviction and psychological truth, the system risks institutionalizing a defense and calling it a choice. Courts need clear decisions. But the mind of a child is not a notarized deed: it is a system of relational survival.

Child-welfare and health services, too, when they lack specific tools for alienation, risk unwitting alliances: they draw close to the more stable narrative, shield the child from the visible conflict, avoid exposure to pain. In doing so they protect the symptom, not the process. They freeze the dynamic instead of transforming it.

The possibility of manipulating a child does not stem from low intelligence, from fragility, or from fault. It stems from the fact that brain and identity are under construction, and that the primary attachment bond is, by definition, non-negotiable. That is why parental alienation must be understood as a process — not as a choice.

In Brief. A child is not a small adult: brain and identity are under construction, and the primary bond is non-negotiable. If even educated adults yield to group pressure and authority, a child can come to believe — authentically — things they never lived. Conviction is not freedom: often, it is protection.

4. Twenty Relational Dynamics of Alienation

The dynamics described in this chapter are the author's original framework, matured through years of field observation, advocacy work, and the analysis of real family and courtroom situations. They are not a reproduction of pre-existing theoretical models but an independent elaboration, developed by integrating international scientific contributions — in particular Baker (2007) on alienating strategies, Harman, Kruk, and Hines (2018) on alienating behaviors as family violence, and Garber (2020) on dynamic rather than diagnostic reading — with direct observation of real situations. These are not abstract theoretical concepts: they are observable relational dynamics which, when they appear in a repeated, consistent, and persistent pattern over time, indicate that a process of alienation is underway.

No single dynamic, taken by itself, is sufficient. It is the whole — the continuity, and the impact on the child — that makes them significant. What makes the difference is not the single episode but the repetition over time, the consistency of the message, and the emotional rigidity that builds up around the child.

What follows describes what the adult does within the relationship. The child does not construct these dynamics: the child adapts to them in order to preserve emotional safety. The child's behaviors, words, and refusals are not the origin of the problem but the result of a relational process that precedes and exceeds them.

Dynamic 1 — Normalized Everyday Disparagement

Everyday disparagement is one of the most insidious dynamics, because it rarely looks violent or explicit. It does not come as open insult but as small repeated phrases, apparently harmless comments, constant insinuations that build up, day after day, a negative image of the other parent.

How it shows itself:

- The alienating parent does not say: "Your dad is a bad person."

They say instead:

- "Your dad — same as always..."
- "Let it go. Your mother doesn't understand these things."

The tone may be ironic, weary, resigned. Precisely for that reason the message slips through unquestioned.

Effect on the child: They slowly absorb the idea that the other parent cannot be trusted — not because they have experienced it, but because that is the story they are told, every day. Their memories say one thing; the adult's words say another. Because they depend emotionally on the parent they live with, they choose to trust the adult's narrative. In time, they stop trusting their own lived experience. They lose contact with what they actually felt, and begin to look at the other parent through someone else's eyes.

Dynamic 2 — The One-Way Narrative

The child is exposed to a single version of the family story, presented as the only true, complete, and morally acceptable one. There is no room for questions, for doubt, for ambivalence.

How it shows itself:

- "I've always done everything on my own."
- "The other one never did anything for you."
- "If you knew what they did to me..."
- "One day you'll understand who they really are."

Every attempt by the child to see the other parent differently is discouraged or met with coldness. The narrative is not offered as a point of view but as absolute truth.

Effect on the child: They learn that understanding is dangerous, that asking questions is risky, that seeing two truths is forbidden. Whenever memories or feelings surface that differ from the received version, they feel a subtle anguish — as if remembering were itself a betrayal.

Dynamic 3 — Protection That Actually Isolates

This dynamic is especially treacherous because it presents itself as care and protection while producing isolation. The alienating parent poses as the one who "knows what is best for the child" and uses fear as a lever to limit the relationship with the other parent.

How it shows itself:

- "Better not to go — they're not stable."
- "I don't want you staying with her. She makes you feel bad."
- "I protect you. He doesn't."
- "You're not safe when you're with him."

The implicit message is powerful: with me you are safe; with the other you are in danger.

Effect on the child: They internalize the idea that contact with the other parent is risky or harmful, even in the absence of any real danger. The refusal is not born of direct negative experience but of anticipated fear: they have been taught to be afraid. And by now, that fear is their own.

Dynamic 4 — Selective Emotional Withdrawal

Selective withdrawal operates at the deepest level of the relationship: access to love. It shows itself as a sudden, targeted change in the parent's emotional bearing whenever the child shows interest in, affection for, or simply mentions the other parent.

How it shows itself: sudden silences, eyes that drop, a stiffening of the body, one-word answers, emotional coldness.

- Child: "I talked to Dad today."
- Parent: (silence, face closing) "Ah."
- Child: "I had fun with Mom."
- Parent: "Good." (cold tone, withdrawal)

Effect on the child: They learn that speaking of the other parent makes love retreat; that showing affection for the other creates distance. For a child, the loss — even temporary — of emotional closeness is an enormous threat. They stop telling. They stop naming. They stop feeling — at least on the surface.

Dynamic 5 — Using the Child as Emotional Support

The boundary between adult and child breaks. Instead of containing the child emotionally, the parent leans on the child. The child becomes the consoler, the confidant, the adult's psychological prop.

How it shows itself:

- "You're the only one who really understands me."
- "I couldn't make it without you."
- "If you leave me, I'll fall apart."
- "You're all I have."

Effect on the child: They feel an enormous responsibility: keeping the parent emotionally standing. They cannot afford to disappoint, to choose freely, to love the other parent without guilt. The refusal of the other parent is not born of anger but of coerced emotional loyalty: "If I see him, I hurt the person who depends on me." This entanglement is profoundly disorganizing for emotional development.

Dynamic 6 — Blurring the Boundary Between the Adult World and the Child's World

The child is drawn into matters that belong to the adult world — legal problems, personal grudges, the details of the separation, money disputes — without the emotional equipment to bear them.

How it shows itself:

- "Do you know what that lawsuit is costing me?"
- "Your father ruined my life."
- "If it weren't for her, we'd be happy."
- "I sacrificed everything for you."

Effect on the child: They feel guilt, hyper-responsibility, fear of betrayal, and lose the ability to tell what belongs to them from what does not. When the boundaries collapse, they are no longer free to be a child. They become witness, ally, judge. And to survive emotionally, they choose the side that feels more fragile or more needful.

Dynamic 7 — Turning the Parent into a Caricature

The rejected parent is no longer described as a real person, with strengths and flaws, but reduced to a stereotyped, simplified, often ridiculed figure. No complexity exists. No ambivalence exists. A label exists.

How it shows itself:

- "Your dad's the one who never gets anything."
- "Your mother ruins everything, always."
- "That's how he is. He'll never change."
- "She's never done a single good thing for anyone."

Effect on the child: They lose the chance to keep positive memories, to recognize real experiences of affection, to integrate the different sides of the relationship. The refusal becomes simple, clean, emotionally "safe." But they learn to split the world into good and bad — and they carry that split inside: if a piece of me comes from that parent, then that piece of me must be bad too.

Dynamic 8 — Systematic Obstruction of Contact

The bond with the other parent is not attacked head-on; it is worn down by absence. Contact is made difficult, irregular, unpredictable — not through explicit prohibition but through everyday obstacles.

How it shows itself:

- "I didn't see the message."
- "You can't go today — you're tired."
- "You're the one who said you didn't want to."
- "Some other time."
- Phone calls that never get passed along.
- Messages "forgotten."
- Visits postponed.
- A last-minute hitch, every time.

Effect on the child: In time, they stop waiting. Then they stop asking. Finally, they stop wanting. The bond weakens not because they chose to break it, but because they were never given the chance to feed it. When the refusal finally surfaces, it looks like their decision. In reality it is the outcome of a relationship left to die slowly.

Dynamic 9 — Rewriting Memory and the Past

The past is progressively edited to make it consistent with the present refusal. Positive memories are not forgotten: they are denied, minimized, or reinterpreted in a negative key.

How it shows itself:

- Child: "I remember when we used to go to the beach with Dad."
- Parent: "Sure — and then he'd always leave you on your own."
- Or: "You remember it wrong. You were never happy there."

The message is subtle but powerful: do not trust your memories. As the literature on reconstructive memory documents (Ceci & Bruck, 1995), children's memories can be significantly altered by the repetition of alternative narratives coming from attachment figures.

Effect on the child: They learn that what they felt is unreliable — that the "right" version is the adult's. Their emotional memory is rewritten to fit the new relational reality, not because the child is lying, but because they need internal coherence: if I reject this parent today, the past must confirm that rejecting him was always right. They lose the continuity of their own story. And with it, a piece of their own identity.

Dynamic 10 — Coerced Loyalty

This is one of the central dynamics of alienation. The child perceives — often without it ever being said aloud — that loving both parents is not possible.

How it shows itself:

- "If you love him, then you don't love me."
- "It hurts me when you go."
- "After everything they did to us..."

The child understands that every gesture of affection toward the other parent has a price: the sadness, anger, silence, or disappointment of the adult they depend on.

Effect on the child: Losing the bond with the parent they live with is an enormous threat. So they choose — not out of freedom, but out of emotional survival. Missing the other parent becomes a dangerous secret, something to hide even from themselves. In time they learn not to feel it anymore — or at least, to believe they don't.

Dynamic 11 — Language That Does Not Fit the Child's Age

A frequent signal of alienating processes is the child's use of words, concepts, and categories that do not belong to their age. The child talks like an adult — sometimes like a consultant.

How it shows itself:

- "My father is manipulative."
- "My mother is a narcissist."
- "He's a toxic person."
- "She doesn't respect my boundaries."

These are expressions that do not come from direct experience but from the absorption of adult language, heard over and over. The child does not recount episodes. The child repeats labels.

Effect on the child: This is not maturity; it is adaptation. They have learned which words "work," which narratives keep the reference adult emotionally steady. Language becomes an instrument of protection, not of expression. When someone asks, "But what exactly did he do to you?", they cannot answer with concrete episodes — because there are none.

Dynamic 12 — The Absence of Emotional Ambivalence

In healthy relationships, even amid conflict, children feel ambivalent emotions: love and anger, affection and disappointment. In alienation, that complexity disappears. One parent is idealized. The other is demonized.

How it shows itself:

- "Mom is perfect."
- "Dad is bad."
- "He's never done anything good."
- "I feel nothing for him. Nothing."

No shades, no positive memories, no contradictions.

Effect on the child: The rigidity is not a sign of emotional clarity: it is a defense mechanism. Holding good and bad together would be destabilizing. Splitting the world into black and white makes them feel safer. But the price is the loss of emotional complexity and inner freedom. They stop feeling authentically and start feeling functionally — only the "permitted" emotions. The others get buried.

Dynamic 13 — Extending the Refusal to the Entire Relational World

The refusal no longer concerns only the parent. It spreads to everything that represents them: grandparents, aunts and uncles, cousins, friends, the excluded parent's new relationships, the places tied to that side of the family.

How it shows itself:

- "I don't want to see Grandma and Grandpa."
- "I don't want to go to their house."
- "I don't like being with those people."
- "They're all on his side."

Effect on the child: The excluded parent's whole relational world is erased in a single block. No alternative bonds remain that might offer a different view of reality. The isolation becomes total. The child lives in a world cut in two, with access to only one half. The other half — which holds people who love them, places they know, memories they own — no longer exists.

Dynamic 14 — Symbolic Replacement of the Parental Role

The rejected parent's role is not merely devalued: it is replaced. New figures are encouraged, explicitly or implicitly, to occupy the parental space left empty.

How it shows itself:

- "Call my partner 'Dad.'"
- "He's your real father."
- "Finally you have a mom who takes care of you."
- "That's not your family anymore."

Effect on the child: They are pushed to transfer the attachment bond, as if relationships were interchangeable. The replacement does not erase the need for the rejected parent: it makes it unspeakable. The child learns that the bond must no longer exist — not even in memory, not even in language. But inside, the void remains. And no replacement fills it.

Dynamic 15 — Minimizing or Denying the Excluded Parent's Pain

The rejected parent's suffering is minimized, mocked, rationalized, or treated as irrelevant.

How it shows itself:

- "If he's suffering, he deserves it."
- "That's her problem."
- "He brought it on himself."
- "I don't care how she's doing."

The child witnesses the progressive dehumanization of the excluded parent.

Effect on the child: It makes the refusal easier and teaches that this pain deserves no empathy. The child learns that feeling compassion is wrong, that recognizing the other's suffering is dangerous, that looking away is safer. But inside, something does not add up: they sense the other's pain is real, and ignoring it takes effort. And that effort consumes them, silently.

Dynamic 16 — Systematic Attribution of Bad Intentions

Every behavior of the rejected parent is read as malicious, regardless of the facts. There are no longer any neutral or ambiguous gestures.

How it shows itself:

- "He only called to check up on you."
- "She does it on purpose to get at me."
- "He gives you presents to manipulate you."
- Child: "Dad sent me a sweet message."
- Parent: "He wants something. Don't fall for it."

Effect on the child: They learn to read reality through a suspicious lens that admits no alternatives. It breeds chronic distrust, an incapacity to rely on others, a fear of being deceived. The rejected parent is no longer seen as a person but as a threat. The child loses the ability to recognize kindness as genuine — in that relationship and, over time, in all the others.

Dynamic 17 — The Illusion of Choice

The child is told, openly or implicitly, that they may choose. On the surface it looks like respect for their will. In reality the emotional field has already been tilted, and the options are not equivalent.

How it shows itself:

- "You decide whether to go... though you know you never feel good there."
- "I won't force you. But you know how I feel."
- "Do what you want... I won't say anything."

The child senses clearly that one choice preserves the emotional balance and the other shatters it.

Effect on the child: This dynamic is especially damaging because it shifts responsibility onto the child, makes them feel like the "author" of a decision that is not free, and exposes them to deep guilt. Over time they internalize: "If I chose it, then it must be right." The coercion becomes invisible. They carry the weight of an enormous responsibility: believing they chose, when they never had a real choice.

Dynamic 18 — Exclusive Emotional Dependence

The bond between child and alienating parent becomes exclusive. The message — rarely spoken, constantly transmitted — is: only I truly understand you; only I know what is right for you; without me, you would suffer.

How it shows itself:

- "Nobody knows you like I do."
- "I always know what you're feeling."
- "With me you can be yourself. With the others you can't."
- "No one else can understand you the way I do."

Effect on the child: They become convinced that no other bond is truly safe and that emotional autonomy is dangerous. Rejecting the other parent becomes the condition for keeping identity and security. The very idea of needing someone else becomes a betrayal.

Dynamic 19 — Denying Time and the History of the Relationship

The past is completely rewritten. Not only are the positive episodes denied: the refusal is presented as having always existed — an original truth.

How it shows itself:

- "You never liked being with him."
- "It's always been like this."
- "Even as a baby, you cried whenever you went."
- "You never had a real relationship."

Effect on the child: They are led to believe the bond was never authentic, that the good memories are illusions, that the present refusal is "natural." The child loses the narrative continuity of their own story. They can no longer say: "It used to be one way, then it changed." They can only say: "It was always like this." Memory is bent to protect the present structure. They feel a void without a name — because part of their life has been erased, and they do not even know they have lost it.

Dynamic 20 — The Loss of the Right to Love Freely

This is the deepest and most destructive dynamic. It is the point where all the others converge.

The child no longer feels permitted to love the other parent. Not because the affection is gone, but because that affection has become guilt, betrayal, danger.

How it shows itself: No explicit phrases are needed anymore. The system is already built. The child knows — without anyone saying it — that loving that parent is not safe. They know it from the silence that falls when they mention him. From the way the look changes. From the tension they feel in the body of the adult beside them.

Effect on the child: They feel a loss they cannot name. It is not grief, because the parent is alive. It is not abandonment, because they were not the one left behind. It is something subtler and more devastating: the sense that part of their world has become unreachable. That loving has become dangerous. That something fundamental has been taken from them — not by force, but by fear.

It is not the loss of a parent. It is the loss of the right to love.

The path of this book continues in Part II, which gives voice to the experience of the targeted parent: the pain, the isolation, the silent struggle to remain present in a child's life.

In Brief. Twenty observable dynamics, from everyday disparagement to the loss of the right to love. No single one proves anything: what counts is repetition over time, the consistency of the message, and the convergence of multiple dynamics from multiple sources. The child does not build them — the child adapts to them.

PART II — THE TARGETED PARENT

5. Disbelief and the Awakening

There is no manual that prepares you for this. There is no course, there is no word that can truly convey the experience of watching your own child look at you as if you were the enemy. Sometimes they do not shout. Sometimes they speak in cold, adult sentences that are not theirs. They tell you things you know do not come from their heart, only from their mouth: they accuse you of wrecking the family, of making the other parent suffer, of being selfish, of never having been there enough. And you listen, and you recognize every word as something that does not belong to them.

You try to explain, and it gets worse. You try to reassure, and they shut down. You try to defend yourself, and that becomes the proof that you really are the bad one. It is a perfect trap: whatever you do is read against you.

And while you struggle to stay calm, not to react, not to wound them, inside you are collapsing. Because you are not losing an argument. You are losing your child, before your own eyes, while you are still here, still alive, still their father or their mother.

The pain is like nothing else. It is not just sadness, not just anger. It is a feeling of unreality, as if your life had suddenly become a story you do not recognize. And this is where the targeted parent enters an unknown land. A land where love is not received but refused. Where presence is experienced as threat. Where the most natural bond in the world becomes something your child appears to need protection from.

If you are reading these pages, it is because in some way you are inside this. And if you are inside it, there is one thing you should know before going on: what you are living is not a fantasy, not an exaggeration, not a weakness. It is the beginning of one of the most painful experiences a parent can endure. And you are not alone.

This is the stage of disbelief. Not of awareness, not of understanding. Of pure bewilderment.

In Brief. The first impact is disbelief: words that do not belong to your child, a trap in which every reaction makes things worse. What you are living is neither exaggeration nor weakness: it is the beginning of one of the most painful experiences a parent can go through. And you are not alone.

6. The Escalation: Accusations, the System, Loss. The Shared Home as a Battlefield

After the request for separation, nothing official happens right away. There is no judge yet, no courtroom, no first hearing. Months pass. A suspended, undefined time, in which you go on living under the same roof, in a space that is no longer a home but is not yet two separate lives. It is in this time that almost everything happens.

The climate hardens. The other parent grows ever more present, intrusive, obsessive. Every gesture is observed, commented on, reinterpreted. Every word becomes evidence. The accusations begin — more and more explicit, more and more harsh. And they are not spoken only between adults: they are spoken in front of the children. And the children listen. Then they begin to repeat — hesitantly at first, then with growing confidence.

You start hearing words you had never heard spoken in that voice. Accusations that do not belong to a child's language, sentences borrowed from an adult world. It is not only what they say. It is how they say it: the tone, the expressions, the look. As if your child were wearing a mask you do not recognize — but whose origin you can guess.

The relationship changes. Respect crumbles. Your authority is contested. The boundaries are turned upside down. In that house you are no longer a parent: you have become the target. And this happens while you are still there, sharing the same rooms, sleeping under the same roof. Time works against you — slow, steady, relentless.

Entering the Court System

After the hearing, for a while, nothing happens on the outside. But inside, everything happens. You walk out of the courtroom feeling that you are no longer inside your own life. The words echo in your head; you function on autopilot. The shock is silent. Then comes the waiting, and with the waiting the fear: fear of being pushed out, fear that the story told about you will become reality simply because it was spoken aloud.

Often a decision arrives that you had not imagined. The child stays with the parent who made the accusations, or you are the one who has to leave. The result is the same: you are physically separated from your child without having chosen it. The silence that follows is devastating. The house is too big, the hours are too long. And your absence is then used as evidence — a cruel paradox.

Custody Evaluations and the Taking of the Bond

Custody evaluations are presented as instruments of clarification and protection. In practice, for the targeted parent, they become one more painful exposure. You suddenly find yourself observed, analyzed, probed — not only as a parent but as a person. The questions reach into your private life, your history, your way of thinking and feeling. Every word is weighed. Every hesitation can become significant. Even the most authentic suffering can be read as instability, rigidity, inadequacy. The sensation is of being placed under a lens that does not look in order to understand, but in order to confirm a story already written elsewhere.

It is often during the evaluation that the gravest passage occurs: the de facto taking of the child. Not always through a dramatic act. Sometimes it happens in an apparently ordinary way: the child is "temporarily" placed with one parent, kept there "for stability," left where they are "pending the evaluation." From that moment, the other parent slowly drops out of the child's daily life. You no longer see them. No longer meet them. No longer hear their voice.

This happens even where a joint custody order formally exists. And it must be said plainly: on paper, custody is shared; in reality, the targeted parent is excluded. At first ambiguously, vaguely. Then more and more openly. You call, and no one answers. You write messages that go nowhere. When someone finally picks up, you are told the child is busy, is doing something else, that this is not a good moment. Sometimes that they are tired. Other times that they don't feel like it. Or that they are upset, that "today is not the day." When the day comes for you to pick them up, you are told the child does not want to come. That their wishes must be respected. That forcing them would be traumatic.

And here comes one of the most painful junctures of the entire process. Because you know — and often everyone knows — that the child is not free to decide. You know that this "will" is not a spontaneous desire but the product of constant pressure, of a manipulated emotional climate. You know the child is not choosing: they are obeying, protecting themselves, repeating. But every attempt to say so is brushed aside. You are told to respect the child, to take a step back, that insisting would make things worse. Day after day, your absence is normalized. Every excuse sounds reasonable; every postponement sounds temporary. But the outcome is usually the same: time passes, and contact never resumes.

Sometimes you discover the child is no longer where you thought. They have been moved to another neighborhood, another house. No international border needs to be crossed for a taking to occur. It is enough to move the child beyond your practical reach. It is an abduction that does not look like an abduction. There are no sirens, no screams, no precise moment you can point to. But for the targeted parent the experience is unmistakable: the child has been taken away. And it happens while the evaluation is still in progress, while you are still formally a parent, while nothing has been established.

Every request for an explanation is deferred: "That will be addressed in the evaluation." "We have to wait." "Let's not force the timeline." But the timeline, meanwhile, works against the bond. The child grows up without seeing you, without hearing you, without experiencing you as a real presence. And the absence is slowly converted into evidence: "See? He's not around." "See? She doesn't take care of them." "See? He doesn't even push for more time." A cruel paradox: you are pushed out — and then accused of not being there.

In the United States, the legal default in most states has long shifted toward joint legal custody and, increasingly, toward broad parenting-time arrangements: courts and statutes proclaim the value of keeping both parents fully involved in a child's life. But a formal allocation of custody says nothing about what actually happens between one hearing and the next. As in every system, the distance between the order on paper and the lived reality of a family can be vast — and it is precisely in that distance that alienating dynamics do their work.

In 2016, FLAGe (Figli Liberi dalla Alienazione Genitoriale — "Children Free from Parental Alienation"), Italy's first national association devoted to parental alienation, founded in 2014 by the author of this book, surveyed a voluntary sample of one hundred parents who had turned to the association over a child's unexplained rejection. The responses showed an essentially balanced distribution: 55 percent fathers and 45 percent mothers among the parents who identified as targeted. Although the sample was non-probabilistic and not nationally representative, the finding points to something the international research confirms: the dynamics of relational exclusion are not structurally tied to one gender. Manipulation can be enacted by mothers and by fathers alike, regardless of which parent the child lives with.

And it is at this point that many parents describe a deep fracture: not only the loss of the child, but the loss of the very possibility of being recognized as a parent. By the time the system decides, the bond has already been severed. When a court order finally arrives, it often looks balanced on paper. Joint custody. Both parents' rights affirmed. Parenting time formally guaranteed. For a moment you think something has been seen — that the relationship with your child can now resume.

But reality is different. What is written on paper takes no account of the time that has passed, of the years of forced absence, of the narrative that has gone on living undisturbed, of the fact that your child has changed. At the beginning they were a child. Then a preteen. Then an adolescent. While justice deliberated, they grew up without you. And so it happens that the child does not come back. Does not come. Does not accept the meeting. Does not answer. At this point it is no longer the other parent saying "they don't want to": it is the child who refuses. This is where the circle closes. You are told that an adolescent cannot be compelled, that their wishes must be respected, that forcing them would do harm. No one seems to remember that this will was formed inside a context of exclusion, that the refusal was born when they were a small child, that for years they had no access to another version of the story. That their emotional identity took shape without you. At this point even the law seems to stop. Not because you have lost the argument, but because time has done its work.

You find yourself facing the most painful form of loss: a loss made "legitimate" by the fact that now it is your child saying no. It is here that many targeted parents come to feel there is nothing practically left to pursue in court — not because remedies do not exist in the abstract, but because time has rendered them ineffective in fact. The toll on mental endurance is enormous. Sleep breaks apart. The body begins to speak: diffuse pain, muscle tension, recurrent headaches, digestive trouble, a chronic exhaustion that no rest relieves.

The Psychological Impact on Targeted Parents

The literature on targeted parents describes a clinically significant impact on mental health, at times comparable to prolonged traumatic stress. National-sample surveys find elevated levels of depression and trauma-related symptoms in targeted parents. In a clinically meaningful share of the sample, indicators of suicide risk emerge that require professional attention (Harman, Leder-Elder & Biringen, 2019). Qualitative studies show that the suffering extends to the fracture of social and personal recognition as a parent, with experiences of helplessness and disorientation (Tavares, Crespo & Ribeiro, 2021; Poustie et al., 2018).

Many targeted parents develop clinically significant psychosomatic symptoms — not out of fragility, but because they are carrying a pain that has no place to be processed. It is a form of protracted traumatic stress: not a sudden collapse, but a daily grinding down.

And what makes everything harder is the absence of recognition. From the outside, the situation often looks "settled": there is an order, there is a custody arrangement, there is a formal frame. But inside, nothing has been repaired.

A methodological note: these studies describe the experience and outcomes of targeted parents; they do not replace clinical-forensic evaluation of the individual case, but they document how frequently severe the psychological burden associated with alienating processes can be.

In Brief. The escalation follows a script: the shared home turned battlefield, accusations spoken in front of the children, entry into the court system, evaluations during which the bond is taken. On paper, custody is joint; in reality the targeted parent is excluded — and the forced absence becomes evidence against them.

7. What Not to Do, and Why

A Parent Under Observation

When you enter the process of alienation, no one tells you a fundamental truth: you are not only under attack — you are being watched while you suffer. Every reaction of yours is read, interpreted, filed away; not to understand you, but to evaluate you. The cruelest paradox is that many of the most instinctive, most human, most understandable reactions are precisely the ones that worsen your position. Not because you are wrong, but because the system — built to weigh facts and observable behavior — often struggles to recognize and handle relational pain when it does not translate into legally typified violations.

Do Not Over-Explain

At the beginning you feel an overwhelming urgency: to explain. To your child, to the caseworkers, to the judge. You have the feeling that if you could only say it right, everything would become clear. It is a natural reaction: the mind seeks order when a bond is being distorted. But in alienation, explaining too much does not clarify: it exposes.

Every explanation is taken apart, lifted out of context, reduced to fragments. Every attempt to tell your side becomes "justification." Every extra word becomes "defensiveness." And your child is not in a position to listen: they are emotionally bound. Every explanation that contradicts the dominant narrative throws them into conflict. And conflict, for a child, is unbearable.

Do Not Defend Yourself in Front of Your Child

When your child accuses you, when they look at you as if you were the guilty one, when they repeat sentences you know are not theirs, the instinct is to defend yourself. To say: "That's not true. That's not how it happened."

But defending yourself in front of them tightens the trap, because it forces them to choose. And a child pushed to an emotional choice will choose the position that lets them survive. The more you defend your truth, the more you are perceived as the attacker — not because you are, but because you are disturbing an equilibrium that, however pathological, is holding them upright. As Warshak (2010) documented, trying to "argue down the programming" with rational explanations often produces a paradoxical effect: the child stiffens further, because the loyalty conflict becomes intolerable. This does not mean accepting false accusations. It means understanding where and when a defense is possible. And in front of your child, at that stage, it is not.

Do Not Chase Contact at Any Cost

As contact shrinks, anxiety rises. And with anxiety comes the chase: you call more often, write longer messages, try to "be there" more. But in alienation, pursuit gets reinterpreted as pressure. Every extra message becomes "intrusiveness." Every attempt becomes "failure to respect boundaries." Every insistence is used to show that you do not know when to stop. While you are searching for your child, the system is taking notes on your behavior.

Do Not React Impulsively to Provocation

The provocations come. From the other parent, from the children, from the professionals. They come as ambiguous remarks, inexplicable decisions, hostile silences. They are subtle provocations, usually deniable. If you react with anger, you are aggressive. If you react with despair, you are unstable. If you react with firmness, you are rigid. Any intense emotional reaction is read as proof of inadequacy.

Do Not Speak Ill of the Other Parent

When you are accused, discredited, erased, the temptation to finally tell the truth is overwhelming. But in alienation, speaking ill of the other parent does not restore balance: it confirms. It confirms the idea that the conflict is mutual, that "they're as bad as each other," that the child is caught between two adults attacking one another. The system does not assess who started it; it assesses who is holding up. And often — unjustly — it scores the composed manipulator higher than the openly suffering target. Baker and Fine (2014) identified the capacity not to respond in kind to provocation as one of the most significant variables for the future recovery of the bond.

Do Not Expect the System to Repair the Bond

This is the most painful disillusionment. The system rarely manages to repair a bond already damaged: it can regulate it, schedule it, sometimes protect it — but it cannot usually rebuild it. It intervenes where there is physical danger, not where there is slow relational destruction. It always arrives afterward. And when it arrives, it often finds a bond already worn thin by time. Expecting it to deliver emotional justice exposes you to a continuous disappointment that erodes you more than an outright refusal would.

Do Not Forget Yourself

Many targeted parents make a silent mistake: they stop living. They put everything on hold — work, relationships, body, future — "until this is resolved." But sometimes it is not resolved on the schedule you imagine. And if you cancel yourself in the waiting, the cost becomes enormous. Remaining a parent does not mean ceasing to exist as a person.

> **In Brief.** You are watched while you suffer, and the most human reactions are the ones that hurt your position most. Do not over-explain, do not defend yourself in front of your child, do not chase contact at any cost, do not answer provocation, do not speak ill of the other parent, do not expect the system to repair the bond. And do not stop existing as a person.

8. Symbolic Erasure and Loneliness

Doubting Yourself

After you have learned to hold back — not to explain, not to defend yourself, not to chase — something happens that is rarely told. You do not collapse, do not explode, do not lash out. Something quieter happens: you begin to doubt yourself. You ask whether you really are the person they describe, whether your child pushed you away because you got something essential wrong, whether in some way you cannot see you were an inadequate parent.

This is one of the most devastating consequences of alienation: not only is your child taken from you — your faith in your own identity as a parent is slowly taken too. The doubt does not come from honest reflection: it comes from constant exposure to a judging gaze that does not know you yet defines you. A gaze that does not enter the complexity, but reduces. That does not see the relationship, but observes its end state and mistakes it for the cause.

When Your Child Stops Calling You Mom or Dad

Then comes one of the most painful moments of all. A moment many parents remember with precision, like a clean wound. Your child stops calling you Dad. Or Mom. They begin calling you by your first name, as if you were just another adult, as if the parental bond had been erased from language before being erased from reality.

"Mom" and "Dad" are not just words. They are a recognition — the sign that, despite everything, the role still exists. When they disappear, you do not lose a form of address: you lose a place in your child's inner world. Being called by your first name is a symbolic erasure: you are no longer positioned as a parent but as a neutral figure, extraneous, without a function. It is a wound that hurts more than an insult, because it does not attack — it deletes.

Often no one grasps the gravity of this passage. People tell you they are only words. But they are not words: they are signs. Signs of a fracture that has occurred inside your child while you were unable to intervene.

Many parents report that from that moment even the child's body changes when they are together. There is no more abandon, no more spontaneity. There is a new stiffness, a guarded gaze, a measured language. As if your child were playing a part. And you see it, you feel it — and you cannot say so, because saying so would unmask a mechanism your child now depends on to stay in balance.

The institutional phrases confirm the erasure. "The child rejects the parent." "Does not recognize him as a reference figure." "Calls her by her first name." Phrases used as evidence rather than as alarm bells — as if the refusal were a free choice and not the outcome of relentless pressure. Then come the phrases that sound protective but certify the loss: "The child's wishes must be respected." "A bond cannot be forced." "The parent should take a step back." Words that ignore the fact that this will was built, that this refusal was born when the child had no tools to defend themselves.

When the Legal Fight Becomes an Attack on Who You Are

Into this scene often steps the other side's attorney — not as a professional of the law, but as someone who turns the proceeding into an attack on your identity. A lawyer who has never met your child, who has never seen your relationship, but who writes briefs soaked in moral judgments and claims that have nothing to do with the child's welfare. Who writes that you are cold, dangerous, unfit. Who uses the fact that your child calls you by your first name as proof of inadequacy, without ever asking why it happened. To strike a parent at the level of identity is to strike the child too. It is to declare that the bond does not deserve protection. The targeted parent reads those pages and feels something give way inside. You are not only attacked as an adult: you are erased as a parent. And you cannot react, because every reaction becomes confirmation. What remains is a loneliness threaded with a sense of injustice that has no voice.

The Loneliness Without a Name

The targeted parent lives a suffering that has no name. The child is not dead, has not disappeared, was not taken by some sudden tragedy. The child is alive, growing, breathing. But no longer there for you. In grief there is an event, a boundary. Here there is none. Every day your child goes on living without you, and you go on living without being able to live them. Every birthday, every holiday, every milestone happens outside your sight. You do not know who they are becoming, what they love, whether they are well. You only know you cannot be there.

Bowlby (1980) described mourning as the response to the interruption of an attachment bond; in alienation the bond is interrupted not by death but by an active erasure — which makes the work of grieving incomparably harder, because the loss is continually reactivated by hope and by the other's existence.

It is a physical pain that shadows everything: an ad seen by chance, a child laughing, an ordinary scene. You cannot shield yourself. Every parent with a child at their side becomes a mirror you did not choose to look into. To this is added a radical loneliness — not the loneliness of having no one around, but of knowing that no one can truly enter that pain.

At first people listen; then they tire; then they tell you to move on, that time fixes everything, that your child will understand one day. Phrases said in good faith that wound more than silence, because none of them accounts for the fact that this bond did not end by choice. It was torn away. Many parents say the hardest part is the evening, when everything stops — no more tasks, no more people, no more roles to play. That is when the absence takes on a body. That is when you feel the weight of everything you did not share: a school day, a difficulty, a laugh, a tiredness. You realize you have no new memories. Living without making new memories with your own child is a profound form of impoverishment.

Time, in this condition, does not heal: it stratifies. Each year adds a layer of distance — not only between you and your child, but between you and the very idea of a future. You live in a suspension that consumes slowly. Many targeted parents say this suffering is worse than mourning. Because in mourning, however immense, the pain can be integrated: you know the other is gone. Here you know they exist — and you cannot reach them. In mourning you can weep openly. Here you often have to stay silent. It is a suspended pain, without a certain end, continually reawakened by hope and by the other's existence. And living suspended is one of the hardest trials the human mind can face.

Protecting Your Child Even as You Lose Them

You cannot share the pain with the one who causes it. You cannot tell your child how much it hurts to be called by your first name, how erased you feel. Because that would make them feel guilty. And you, despite everything, keep protecting them. This is one of the most harrowing contradictions of alienation: you protect your child even as they are losing you.

The Guilt of Not Being Able to Save Them

There is a pain inside the pain that almost no one names. A pain that is not about you, not about your need to be a parent, not about wounded pride. It is about your child. About the fact that you see them suffering — and can do nothing.

Because you know. You know with a certainty that steals your sleep. You know that the confidence they display is not serenity. That the rigidity is not strength. That the refusal they voice is born not of freedom but of fear. You know them better than anyone. You saw their eyes when they could still let go. You felt their body relax against yours. You knew the child before the mask.

And now you look at them — when you are allowed to look — and you see something that devastates you: a child paying an enormous price for a war they did not choose. A child who had to give up part of themselves to survive emotionally. A child who built an armor so perfect that everyone thinks they are fine — and you know that inside that armor there is someone who can no longer feel. The guilt you carry is not rational. You know that. You are not the cause. You did not build that prison. But guilt does not follow logic; it follows love. And a parent's love says only one thing: I should be able to protect them. And I cannot.

You wonder what happens when they cry and you are not there. Whether anyone notices when they pretend. Whether at night, in the dark, when the mask is no longer needed, they miss you — and whether missing you hurts them the way it hurts you. You wonder whether they are developing anxiety. Whether they have nightmares. Whether their friendships are what they seem, or whether they have learned to control those too. You wonder whether one day they will pay the price for all of this — in adolescence, in adult relationships, in the capacity to trust, to love, to let go.

And the answer — the one you know and do not want to look at — is: yes. Probably yes. The consequences will come. Not now, perhaps. But they will come. Because a child who was asked to erase a parent in order to survive does not emerge from that experience untouched.

And the question hangs there: what traces will all this leave over time? Empirical research confirms that childhood exposure to alienating behaviors is associated with significant long-term psychological outcomes. In a study published in *The American Journal of Family Therapy*, Baker and Verrocchio (2016) found that adults who had lived through alienating dynamics as children reported significantly higher levels of anxiety and depression than non-exposed subjects. It is a statistical association, not an inevitable destiny — but the finding suggests that the forced exclusion of an attachment figure can leave lasting marks on emotional regulation.

You intuit these things. You do not need to read them in a study. You feel them in your body every time you think of your child. And the cruelest part is this: you have the emotional skills to help them. You are the parent who could offer them the space to feel, to doubt, to cry, to be ambivalent without fear. But you cannot reach them. You are not allowed. The helplessness you feel is not passivity. It is the condition of someone watching damage unfold with no instruments to intervene. It is like watching your child through glass: you see them, but you cannot touch them. You can pound on the glass, you can shout, you can weep — the glass does not break. And on the other side, your child has learned not to look your way.

This helplessness produces a specific effect on the mind: a chronic, muffled guilt that does not ease with time. Not the guilt of having done something wrong, but the guilt of having failed to prevent something wrong. It is the guilt of the parent who knows, who sees, who understands — and who cannot act.

A guilt the outside world does not recognize, because the outside world sees a child who "seems fine" and a parent who "is no longer around." Many targeted parents say this is the deepest wound: not their own suffering, but their child's. Not the exclusion endured, but the impossibility of protecting. Because you can learn to live with your own pain. What you never learn is to live with your child's pain when you can do nothing to ease it.

If you are reading these lines and feel they describe exactly what you are living, know this: that guilt does not belong to you. It is not yours. It is the product of a system that stripped you of the means to exercise the most natural function there is: caring for the person you brought into the world. The fact that you feel this guilt is not a sign of weakness. It is the sign that you are still, profoundly, a parent. And that your love, even when it cannot act, has never stopped seeing.

The Silent Resistance

And yet, you remain. You remain faithful to who you were as a parent. You stay clear of revenge, of destruction. You hold an ethical position no one gives you credit for, but which you feel is the only one possible. Remaining like this is not passivity: it is a form of silent resistance. The suffering you are living is not pathological, not excessive, not weakness. It is the human price of a bond torn away without consent.

The hope that remains is not luminous or consoling. It is the possibility that, growing up, your child will begin to feel cracks in the narrative they were immersed in. That adolescence, or adult life, will open a distance from the alienating parent. That questions will arise. Baker (2007), analyzing the accounts of adults exposed as children to alienating dynamics, observed that some of them describe a process of re-elaboration and, at times, of reconnection with the previously rejected parent — often coinciding with independent adult life and the building of autonomous relationships.

Alongside that hope lives a painful awareness the targeted parent carries in silence: the consequences of what the child has lived will surface later — not now, not while they are still protected by the rigidity of the narrative, but when life demands autonomy, responsibility, and the construction of identity. To know this, without being able to protect them, is one of the hardest forms of love.

To remain a parent, in these cases, does not mean waiting for a return. It means not betraying what you have become as a parent. It means not letting the violence you suffered turn you into someone you do not recognize. To have come this far without breaking entirely is not a given. It is a form of resistance no one talks about. A silent endurance with no applause and no medals.

If you have read this far, you are not fragile. If you are still standing, you are not weak. If you go on loving despite everything, you are not naive. The rest does not depend only on you. Staying true to yourself does.

The path continues in Part III, where the gaze shifts to the one who drives the alienation: how the alienating parent functions — without indulgence and without caricature.

In Brief. When your child stops calling you Mom or Dad, you do not lose a word: you lose a place in their inner world. It is mourning without a death, continually reawakened by hope. The guilt you feel — seeing the harm and being unable to stop it — is not yours: it is the sign that you are still, profoundly, a parent.

PART III — THE ALIENATING PARENT

9. Who the Alienating Parent Is

The alienating parent is someone who, in everyday life, can appear normal, functional, even charming. They work, they socialize, they present well. They are often persuasive — often the first person in a room to win people's sympathy. This is precisely why they are so hard to recognize.

The Past That Precedes the Alienation

When we observe the functioning of someone who enacts alienating dynamics, the temptation is to stop at the visible behavior: the control, the devaluation, the one-sided narrative, the emotional rigidity. But no behavior is born in a vacuum. Every relational pattern has roots in a history.

Often the parent who cannot tolerate separation does not come from an explicitly violent or dramatic background. Sometimes they come from apparently "normal" families where love was nevertheless conditional, performance was rewarded over authenticity, and approval was fragile. In these histories, the child learns early that to be seen they must measure up, that to be loved they must meet expectations, that personal worth is not intrinsic but negotiable. Other times the past is marked by emotional instability: unpredictable parents, alternating warmth and coldness, intermittent presences. The child grows up developing an acute sensitivity to abandonment, a constant radar for signals of distance, a deep fear of being left. Under these conditions, the bond is not only affection: it is survival. Bowlby (1969–1980) described how the internal working models built in childhood tend to reactivate the same attachment patterns in moments of adult crisis; marital separation is one of those moments.

It is not unusual for the future alienating parent to have been, in their own childhood, a child forced to adapt early. A child who learned to read the adult's mood to avoid conflict, to control the environment in order to feel safe, to construct a self-image that was strong, competent, unassailable. Self-esteem, in these cases, is not stable ground: it is a construction that requires continuous confirmation. Growing up, this structure can turn into an intense need for relational control. Not out of deliberate dominance, but out of fear.

Separation, in this picture, is not simply the end of a relationship: it is the reactivation of an old experience of loss, devaluation, invisibility. It is the resurfacing of a wound that was never fully worked through.

Separation as a Wound to Identity

It must be said clearly: the person who enacts alienating dynamics rarely experiences themselves as a manipulator. More often they perceive themselves as wounded. Betrayed. As the one who must protect themselves and the child from an injustice.

The narrative they construct is not always cynical: it is defensive. As Baker and Fine (2014) observed, alienating parents typically show little awareness of the impact of their behavior on the child, perceiving themselves as protectors rather than agents of harm. Looking at this origin means reading the dynamic with a wider lens, able to distinguish between conscious intent and defensive reaction. To understand the alienating parent you have to look where no one looks: not at individual acts, but at the overall functioning — at how they perceive themselves, the other, and the relationship. The starting point is always the same: the end of the couple is experienced not as a painful relational event, but as a wound to identity. The alienating parent does not lose a partner: they lose a part of themselves.

The couple relationship was not a space between two autonomous people; it was the pillar holding up their self-image. This is why the separation is not processed as a loss to be crossed, but as an attack to be defended against.

Here the fundamental distortion is produced: the inability to distinguish the end of the couple from the destruction of the Self. The alienating parent cannot conceive that the marital bond can end without annihilating their personal worth — that parenting can and must survive the end of the relationship. This confusion generates an intense defensive reaction: rage, resentment, a need for redress.

The pain is not recognized as an internal experience; it is externalized and attributed to the other parent, who becomes the one who "destroyed the family," "betrayed the pact," "ruined everything." Even in the absence of a new relationship, the alienating parent is convinced that the separation must conceal "someone else," real or imagined. The history of the couple is reread retroactively to confirm this conviction.

The rejection is experienced as intolerable and produces a defensive reaction that oscillates between victimhood and rage. The other parent is not recognized as a person exercising a right of self-determination, but as the one who "destroyed everything."

And the pain, unable to be recognized as a legitimate emotion, turns into hostility. The suffering is converted into accusations, suspicion, control, and the need for payback. This passage marks the beginning of the alienating dynamic proper.

How the Manipulation Works

The alienating parent's manipulation is not chaotic. It has a structure, an internal logic, a coherence that holds over time. It is not an emotional reaction that gets out of hand; it is a relational functioning that activates every time the other parent expresses discomfort, sets a limit, claims respect, or shows autonomy.

The Reversal of Reality

The first mechanism is the most destabilizing: the reversal of responsibility. When the other parent points out that they have been mistreated, devalued, or disrespected, the response is neither listening nor reflection — it is the rewriting of the scene. The content of the complaint is erased and replaced with a new narrative, in which the alienating parent positions themselves as the victim and the other as the culprit. The person on the receiving end feels they are losing their mind: every time they try to say "you hurt me," they find themselves defending against an accusation that did not exist a minute earlier.

Baseless Accusations

The alienating parent's accusations are not grounded in verifiable facts. They change object over time but keep an unchanged structure and return cyclically. The other parent is accused of real or imagined betrayals, ulterior motives, hidden intentions. The accusations have no clarifying function: they serve to delegitimize the other's word, to produce a state of constant defense, to shift the center of gravity from the alienating parent's responsibility to the other's presumed behavior.

Pathological Jealousy

In the alienating parent, jealousy is not an emotional reaction proportionate to a real event. It is a stable, pervasive structure, marked by chronic suspicion, projection, and the need for control. The rigid premise: the other cannot be free without being guilty. Every neutral behavior — new activities, social relationships, personal growth — is reinterpreted as indirect proof of disloyalty. The absence of objective evidence does not weaken the suspicion; it strengthens it, because subjective conviction takes on the value of absolute truth.

When a suspicion is disproven, no reassurance follows: the accusatory object simply shifts to new figures or situations. What stays constant is not the person suspected, but the accusatory structure. The recurring lines — "I know you're hiding something from me," "There's no way you just left like that," "You're doing this on purpose to make me suffer" — instill doubt, guilt, and an obligation of continuous self-justification. Every attempt at clarification is reinterpreted as further proof of deception.

The Victim Position

It is not a transient reaction tied to the pain of separation. It is a stable identity structure that organizes how the person perceives themselves, the other, and the entire relational reality. Reality is simplified into a rigid, polarized scheme: I gave everything, the other destroyed everything. Every attempt at dialogue is experienced as a personal attack. The lines — "You destroyed the family," "After everything I did for you," "The kids are suffering because of you" — are not momentary outbursts. They are bricks in a narrative that is built, repeated, and consolidated until it becomes the official truth of the separation.

The Appropriation of Worth

A less visible but deeply erosive mechanism: the other parent's professional achievements, personal growth, skills, and successes are attributed to one's own intervention or influence. The underlying message: "Without me, you wouldn't be who you are." It reinforces emotional dependence and makes leaving the relationship harder.

The Absence of Repair

The accusatory cycle never ends in real repair. There is no taking of responsibility, no authentic apology, no stable change. The phases of apparent calm are temporary suspensions of the pattern, which reactivates as soon as the other parent reasserts themselves. The other parent, progressively, tends to over-justify, to doubt their own perception, to shrink their emotional expression.

This adaptation is not a sign of guilt: it is relational survival in an invalidating context.

> **In Brief.** The alienating parent rarely experiences themselves as a manipulator: they feel wounded, betrayed, protective. The separation is not processed as a loss but as an attack on identity, and the unrecognized pain converts into hostility: reversal of reality, cyclical accusations, jealousy, victimhood, appropriation of worth. And no repair, ever.

10. The Mechanisms of Manipulation and Personality Traits

The behaviors described are not mere emotional reactions contingent on the separation. They sit within a relatively stable personality functioning — not a clinical diagnosis, but a psychological configuration that recurrently organizes how the person perceives themselves, the other, and relationships. In the psychodynamic field, Otto Kernberg (1975) described how personality organizations marked by narcissistic fragility and relational instability tend to activate rigid defenses in situations of loss or threat to self-image. Under such conditions, separation can intensify defensive patterns already present, amplifying mechanisms of devaluation, projection, and polarization.

Vulnerable Narcissism

Narcissistic traits do not necessarily express themselves in grandiose or openly dominant forms. More often they take a vulnerable configuration: a constant need for confirmation, recognition, and external legitimation. In these configurations, the sense of personal worth is not internally stabilized but depends to a significant degree on the gaze of the other. Being right, occupying a position of moral superiority, being recognized as the injured party becomes essential to maintaining internal coherence.

The literature has long distinguished grandiose from vulnerable narcissism, noting that the latter is marked by hypersensitivity to criticism, fragile self-esteem, and intense emotional reactivity to experiences of rejection (Pincus & Lukowitsky, 2010; APA, DSM-5-TR).

Separation can represent, in this picture, a particularly intense narcissistic injury. It is not experienced as a shared relational loss, but as an intolerable personal rejection. The pain does not easily find space for internal processing and tends to transform into rage, grievance, and a need for symbolic redress.

Every limit set by the other is perceived as an affront, every autonomous choice as an attack, every act of differentiation as betrayal. In dynamic terms, the end of the relationship reactivates experiences of devaluation that threaten the ideal self-image (Kernberg, 1975).

When expectations of recognition go unmet, a mechanism of devaluation of the other can activate. The relational world tends to organize in a polarized way:

whoever confirms is loyal and right; whoever does not confirm is ungrateful or hostile. Empathic capacity may also be reduced — not from a total absence of emotion, but from difficulty recognizing and legitimizing internal states that do not coincide with one's own needs.

The other's reactions are reinterpreted through the filter of the narcissistic wound: pain becomes manipulation, silence becomes threat, distance becomes indifference. Taking responsibility is often the most delicate point: admitting a mistake would crack the internal image of coherence and legitimacy. So blame tends to be projected outward.

In a high-conflict separation, these dynamics can favor the delegitimization of the other parent and turn the child into a privileged source of confirmation: the child's rejection of the other parent can be experienced as indirect proof of one's own "rightness." Understanding this functioning does not mean justifying its effects, but recognizing that, where narcissistic vulnerability is present, separation can trigger intense defensive responses with direct repercussions on the family system.

Relational Paranoia

In some cases paranoid traits may be present — understood not as a psychotic condition but as a stable mode of interpreting relational reality. It is a functioning marked by persistent suspicion, distrust, and a persecutory reading of others' intentions.

The attributions are not primarily grounded in objective evidence, but in an internal structure that makes it hard to tolerate uncertainty, ambivalence, and above all the other's autonomy.

The ex-partner is observed through a rigid interpretive lens: every behavior, however neutral, is loaded with hidden meanings. An unanswered message becomes proof of hostility. A delay becomes intent. A new relationship becomes retroactive betrayal.

Separation amplifies this configuration: the loss of access and predictability is experienced as threat, and the need for control translates into over-interpretation. A central element of this functioning is unshakeable subjective conviction. Hypotheses are not formulated: the suspicion is experienced as certainty.

One's own emotional perceptions take on the value of evidence. The other's clarification does not reduce the doubt, because the doubt does not arise from a lack of information but from an internal structure of interpretation. Cognitive psychology has described how, in paranoid patterns, selective hyperattention and confirmation bias tend to amplify the elements consistent with the suspicion and to ignore those that might contradict it (Freeman, 2007; APA, DSM-5-TR). In a high-conflict separation, this functioning can transform conflict into perceived persecution.

The other parent is no longer a person with whom a relationship has ended, but a potentially hostile figure to defend against. The child, placed inside this interpretive frame, can be drawn in as an ally or witness to the presumed threat. When reality is filtered through a stable persecutory lens, the conflict tends to harden and become impervious to discussion: not because arguments are lacking, but because the interpretive system does not allow for the possibility of being wrong.

Relational Instability

In some cases there may be traits of marked emotional and relational instability, which intensify at moments of loss or separation. The end of the couple is not experienced as a painful but passable process: it takes the form of a sudden, total, intolerable rupture.

It is not only the relationship that ends: the very sense of internal continuity falters. The separation reactivates deep experiences of abandonment, exclusion, and devaluation that may have roots far older than the current relationship. In these configurations, the other parent may be idealized in some phases and rapidly devalued in others, with no real emotional continuity.

The bond is perceived in polarized terms: total fusion or definitive rupture. Regulated distance — the possibility of staying in relationship while different — becomes hard to tolerate.

The clinical literature on borderline personality organization describes relational patterns marked precisely by oscillations between idealization and devaluation, intense sensitivity to abandonment, and affective instability that amplifies in situations of separation (Kernberg, 1975; Gunderson, 2001; APA, DSM-5-TR).

When this instability activates in the context of a high-conflict separation, the conflict does not stay confined to the couple. The adult's anguish seeks regulation elsewhere. The child can be invested — often not fully consciously — with the task of stabilizing the parent's emotional equilibrium. It is not necessarily a deliberate choice, but a dynamic in which the child becomes an anchoring figure, called on to fill emotional voids the adult struggles to sustain alone.

Where marked relational instability is present, separation can thus turn from a painful event into a disorganizing experience, with direct repercussions on where the child is placed within the adult's emotional system.

Defensive Rigidity

Defensive rigidity is the structural inability to modify one's positions in the face of experience, discussion, or the evidence of facts.

Every change of perspective is experienced not as enrichment but as threat. This is not simple stubbornness of character, but a deep defensive mode: revising one's position would mean cracking the internal self-image, tolerating doubt, admitting possible responsibility. In this functioning, discussion is not dialogue but attack.

Contrary evidence does not open a space for reflection: it is reinterpreted, minimized, or neutralized. Internal coherence matters more than external reality. Not because there is a deliberate intent to distort the facts, but because psychological stability depends on the rigidity of the narrative. If that narrative gives way, so does the emotional equilibrium it sustains.

Defensive rigidity often shows itself as absolute certainty: the parent does not say "I could be wrong," but "I know how things are." Nuances are perceived as dangerous ambiguities. Ambivalence is intolerable. In a separation, this mode makes it impossible to distinguish between the couple's conflict and the parenting function: every disagreement becomes proof of the other's guilt, every limit set is read as hostility.

When this structure consolidates, even outside intervention struggles to make a dent. Not because tools are lacking, but because change would require an internal revision the defensive system does not allow. In this frame, the alienating narrative is not merely a strategy: it becomes a psychological necessity of stabilization.

Recognizing it for what it is — not stubbornness of character but a defensive structure — helps explain why every attempt at mediation risks hitting a wall that is not ideological but structural. The contemporary literature frames it as psychological inflexibility: the difficulty of revising one's interpretations even when experience suggests an update (Kashdan & Rottenberg, 2010). From a psychodynamic perspective, research on defense mechanisms has shown that the quality and modifiability of a person's defensive configuration are closely correlated with developmental and relational outcomes over time (Vaillant, 1986).

The Incapacity to Mentalize

A deep trait that can sustain alienating functioning is impaired mentalization: the capacity to recognize one's own and others' mental states as distinct, subjective, and potentially different. Fonagy and colleagues (2002) define mentalization as the ability to understand behavior — one's own and others' — in light of intentions, emotions, and internal representations.

When this capacity is fragile, the other is not perceived as a separate person with an autonomous mind, but as an extension, a threat, or an antagonist. In this configuration, the other parent's actions are not interpreted as expressions of complex inner experience, but as intentional acts aimed at causing harm. A confusion between emotion and reality is observed: if I feel anger, then the other is guilty; if I feel fear, then the other is dangerous; if I feel hurt, the other did it deliberately. Subjective perception takes on the value of objective proof.

This fragility also compromises the relationship with the child. The parent struggles to recognize the child's emotional needs as separate from their own and tends to read the child's reactions in terms of their own narrative.

The child's emotions are not received as autonomous expressions of an inner world in formation, but interpreted as confirmations, alliances, or betrayals. The developmental risk, in these contexts, is a compromised process of differentiation and individuation in the child.

The Delusional Configuration with Preserved Reality Contact

In the most severe cases, a rigid, self-sustaining configuration of relational reality can emerge. This is not necessarily a generalized psychotic delusion, but a delusional core confined to the relationship with the ex-partner.

The psychodynamic literature describes these configurations as partial paranoid organizations (Kernberg, 1975): belief systems that are coherent, logically structured, impervious to refutation, yet limited to specific relational domains.

The parent can appear lucid, functional, and well-adapted in other areas of life. It is precisely this apparent normality that makes the dynamic hard to recognize. Within the relational narrative, however, every event is reinterpreted consistently with a core conviction: the other is a persecutor, a betrayer, or a danger.

Disconfirmations produce no revision. They are integrated as further proof of deception or manipulation. The narrative structure becomes self-sealing: nothing cracks it, everything confirms it. In these configurations, the risk is that the child is progressively drawn inside the same rigid interpretive frame.

Chronic Lying and Narrative Reorganization

In some configurations, a systematic reorganization of reality is observed through omissions, selections, and reformulations of the facts. This is not occasional lying, but a persistent narrative adaptation. Autobiographical memory is not a neutral archive; it is a dynamic system. Studies of memory reconstruction (Loftus, 1997) show that memories can be reorganized to serve the identity and defensive needs of the present.

In alienating functioning, this process can take a structured form: complex events are simplified, incongruent elements are removed, neutral episodes are reinterpreted retroactively, and omissions become as central as assertions.

A characteristic element is a reduced perception of guilt. The falsification is not experienced as deception, but as legitimate defense or necessary protection. Over time, the reconstructed narrative is integrated into personal identity until it is perceived as fully authentic truth.

This process does not necessarily imply conscious bad faith. Often it is a defensive adaptation that protects narcissistic integrity and the internal coherence of the Self.

Levels of Severity

Alienating functioning does not show itself the same way in every case.

At mild levels, the parent shows some awareness of the conflict, can partially accept discussion, and the child maintains an ambivalent but present bond with both parents. Timely intervention can make the difference.

At moderate levels, the narrative stiffens, cooperation becomes difficult, and moralized language begins to appear.

At severe levels, the rejection is rigid and without ambivalence, the narrative is impervious to any contrary evidence, the parent actively recruits third parties and may produce instrumental false accusations; the child reproduces the adult's language as if it were their own.

At extreme levels, there is complete exclusion of the other parent from the child's life, delusional functioning with preserved reality contact, systematic manipulation of institutions, and developmental harm already underway. In these cases, time works against the child, and every delay consolidates the damage.

Recognizing alienating functioning is not labeling or simplifying. It serves an essential purpose: making legible what, if unnamed, keeps operating. It is from this legibility that any real protection of the child can begin.

In Brief. Beneath the behaviors lies a functioning: vulnerable narcissism, a persecutory reading of reality, relational instability, defensive rigidity, fragile mentalization, up to the circumscribed delusional core and the lie that becomes identity. The levels of severity — mild, moderate, severe, extreme — set the urgency of intervention.

11. Revenge Through the Children and Its Consequences

How Children Become Instruments

In the alienating parent's functioning, revenge is not expressed mainly through direct attacks on the ex-partner. It takes a more indirect and more devastating form: the use of the children as instruments of emotional regulation, narcissistic repair, and relational payback. The children are not drawn in by accident. They become the place where unprocessed pain, rage, and humiliation find an acceptable form of expression — often disguised as protection, concern, or parental love.

Striking the other parent through the children makes it possible to keep control, moral superiority, and an apparently legitimate position. The children are progressively loaded with improper functions. They can become emotional consolers, confirmations of the parent's innocence, implicit allies, witnesses to the wrong suffered, instruments of pressure. The child is no longer seen as a person with needs of their own, but as an emotional resource.

The delegitimization of the other parent proceeds through devaluing comments, doubts cast on parenting abilities, the portrayal of the other as dangerous. Often it is not explicit: it shows itself through insinuations, silences, sighs, glances, or selective stories that steer the child's perception without requiring any declared stance.

The most insidious aspect is that the revenge is almost always presented as a protective act. The lines that give it away: "I only think about the children's well-being." "I can't force them to see you." "I don't want them to suffer the way I did." "One day they'll understand who you really are."

These expressions moralize the conflict, legitimize the exclusion of the other parent, and shift attention from the relational dynamic to the child's presumed good. Protection becomes a rationalization of revenge. Alienation produces deep and lasting effects because it exposes the child to a conflict that does not belong to their developmental path, yet is handed to them as an improper emotional task. The child is not a mere spectator of the dynamic: they become an active part of the relational system, often without the tools to understand its meaning or its consequences.

Identity Confusion

Because the child is biologically and psychologically bound to both parents, the systematic devaluation of one of them produces an internal fracture. The attack on one parent is experienced, at a deep level, as an attack on a part of the self.

The child struggles to answer fundamental questions: who am I, where do I come from, whom can I resemble without feeling guilty. They may shift attitudes and stories depending on the context, adapting to whichever parent is present, until they progressively lose contact with a stable, coherent perception of their own identity.

Guilt and Parentification

The guilt does not arise from genuinely harmful behavior, but from an implicit attribution of emotional responsibility: loving the other parent, wanting their presence, or feeling their absence amounts to causing suffering.

Guilt thus becomes an internal regulating mechanism that steers behavior without the need for explicit demands. Parentification appears when the child is drawn into functions that are not theirs: supporting, consoling, emotionally protecting the alienating parent. Garber (2020) describes this configuration as dyadic enmeshment: a fusion between the adult's needs and the child's role that compromises the process of individuation. This role reversal can be mistaken for early maturity; in reality it represents a forced surrender of one's position as a child.

The Effects Over Time

In the medium and long term, the alienation experience can affect the capacity to trust, the building of intimate relationships, the handling of conflict, and the fear of abandonment.

In a retrospective study of adults who as children had reported exposure to alienating behaviors, Baker (2007) found significant rates of depression (70%), low self-esteem (56.3%), difficulty trusting (54.2%), and substance abuse (35.4%). These are data from self-reported samples, not generalizable in an epidemiological sense, but they indicate a clinically relevant tendency: prolonged exposure to alienating dynamics can be associated with problematic emotional and relational outcomes in adulthood.

The forms the distress takes are varied: the apparently mature child who gave up their childhood early; the rejecting child, with rigid convictions and adult language; the silent child, who expresses the conflict through the body — sleep disturbances, regressions, withdrawal. These are not deliberately hostile choices: they are survival strategies.

The System That Does Not Change on Its Own

Taken together, these elements — the inability to accept the separation, defensive rigidity, pathological jealousy, the victim position, the use of the child as an emotional regulator — are not a random sequence of reactions. They form a closed, self-referential relational system, resistant to outside reality.

The alienating parent is not looking for a solution to the conflict: they are looking for confirmation of their narrative. Until that narrative is challenged by competent and timely outside intervention, the system tends to perpetuate and reinforce itself.

How to Distinguish Alienation from Conflict

As illustrated in Chapter 2, the difference between ordinary post-separation conflict and parental alienation is not quantitative but qualitative and structural. It is worth recalling here, in the context of concrete indicators.

In ordinary post-separation conflict, even when heated, the child maintains emotional ambivalence: they can be angry with one parent and affectionate with the other, can swing back and forth, can express contradictory emotions. The emotions are fluid, not rigid. The rejection, when present, is situational and often reactive to specific episodes. With time and appropriate intervention, the bond can settle, and repair is possible.

In alienation, the rejection takes on different characteristics: it becomes global, rigid, moralized. The rejected parent is not simply "the one I'm angry with," but becomes "the wrong one," "the bad one," "the dangerous one." The narrative is one-sided and impervious to doubt. Time, rather than easing the emotional position, consolidates the rejection. As Fidler and Bala (2010) observe, distinguishing high-intensity conflict from alienation requires a longitudinal analysis of the family dynamic: a single episode or a single statement by the child is not enough. One must assess the persistence over time of specific indicators, the consistency of the relational pattern, and the evolution — or failure to evolve — of the rejection.

The clinical literature further notes that in alienation cases the child often presents adult, moralized language, absence of ambivalence, rejection extended even to the excluded parent's extended family, and justifications that are weak or disproportionate to the severity of the rejection (Baker, 2007; Warshak, 2010). These features are not typically found in ordinary conflicts, where the child retains spaces of affection, positive memories, and the possibility of revision.

Alienation, then, is not recognized in the snapshot but over time. Not in the single argument, but in the stabilization of a pattern: an unchanging narrative, no accountability assigned to the favored parent, rigidity of the rejection, exclusive alignment with one parental figure, and systematic obstruction of the relationship with the other. In conflict you observe tension. In alienation you observe crystallization. And it is this crystallization — not the emotional intensity — that is the most reliable indicator for the clinical and forensic distinction.

The Errors of Evaluators

The professional facing an alienation case risks specific errors.

The first is false evenhandedness: treating both parents as equally responsible, regardless of the behaviors observed. It looks neutral, but it is clinically wrong: it legitimizes the dysfunctional behavior, blames the targeted parent, and confuses the child. Neutrality does not imply symmetry. An equally serious error is attributing the rejection to the child's autonomous choice. This reading ignores the mechanisms of forced loyalty, assigns the child an improper responsibility, and consolidates the rejection as a "right." Alienated rejection is not a free choice: it is an adaptive strategy in a coercive context. The targeted parent is often misread: interpreted as overly defensive, overactive, emotionally unstable. Their behaviors, instead of being read as outcomes of the invalidating dynamic, are treated as the cause of the child's rejection. It is a short circuit that deepens the victim's isolation.

Mediation in Contexts of Parental Alienation

Family mediation is a valuable instrument in many separation conflicts; it is inadequate where structured alienation is present.

In parental alienation contexts, mediation is often proposed as a neutral tool for resolving the conflict. In the abstract, mediation presupposes two fundamental conditions: the parties' good faith and a minimum basis of communicative reciprocity.

These premises are structurally absent when the conflict is not symmetrical but organized around manipulative, coercive, and controlling dynamics. Where one parent shows marked narcissistic traits or a functioning centered on domination and devaluation of the other, mediation is not a ground for negotiation but a further arena for the exercise of power.

The very logic of mediation — "meeting halfway," acknowledging mutual responsibilities, finding a compromise — becomes paradoxical when one of the two parents is not interested in cooperation but in the destruction of the other's bond with the child. In such configurations, the mediation table risks turning into a performative stage: the alienating parent can present as reasonable, collaborative, even victimized, while keeping the real dynamics of manipulation of the child outside the room.

The result is a perceptual distortion that can lead the mediator to read the conflict as bidirectional and symmetrical, when it is in fact a marked relational asymmetry.

To say that "you cannot mediate with a narcissist" is not a rhetorical formula but a clinical-relational datum: mediation presupposes the capacity to mentalize, to take responsibility, and to recognize the other as a separate person. In a rigid narcissistic configuration, the other is experienced as an extension or a threat; the child becomes an object of instrumental alliance; the conflict is fed because it serves the maintenance of control. In this scenario, mediation is not only ineffective: it can help chronify the problem, offering the alienating parent yet another arena of legitimation.

Particularly critical is the prospect of mandatory, fee-based mediation in high-conflict separations. Applied indiscriminately to parental alienation contexts, such a requirement is deeply inadequate on two grounds: clinical and socioeconomic.

On the clinical level, a blanket mandate skips the preliminary assessment of the nature of the conflict. Not all conflicts are mediable. Where structured manipulative dynamics, denigration campaigns, systematic obstruction of parenting time, and the child's recruitment into exclusive alliances are present, the priority is not negotiation between adults but the protection of the child's right to both parents and to freedom from psychological pressure.

Forcing mediation under these conditions means losing precious time — and in alienating processes, time is a clinically decisive variable. The more time passes, the more the child's rejection crystallizes and consolidates into relational identity.

What is anesthetized does not disappear. It stays beneath the surface, ready to resurface in other forms: somatic symptoms, relational difficulties, affective rigidity, unnamed emotional voids.

Mandatory mediation in parental alienation cases is also socioeconomically inadequate, because it adds costs in contexts already burdened by heavy litigation expenses — attorneys' fees, custody evaluations, expert witnesses, court costs.

Where economic asymmetries exist, it risks penalizing the more fragile parent, who may be pushed to accept unfavorable agreements to contain expenses, while the other party can use it for delay. Since in these cases the conflict is structural, mediation has low odds of success and often adds itself to, without replacing, the court proceeding — creating a double cost. Over the medium to long term, this makes the process financially unsustainable and compromises equal access to judicial protection.

So far, the functioning of the adult who alienates. But it is on the child that this functioning deposits its effects: adaptive configurations, defenses built not to wound but to keep from collapsing. Understanding them serves to avoid the gravest error: mistaking an adaptation for a choice.

In Part IV the gaze shifts to the alienated child: the wounds they carry, the survival strategies they adopt, and the consequences that remain.

In Brief. The revenge passes through the children and presents itself as protection. Conflict differs from alienation in one thing: in conflict there is ambivalence, in alienation crystallization. This is why mediation, valuable elsewhere, is inadequate in structured cases: you cannot mediate with someone who seeks the destruction of the bond.

PART IV — THE ALIENATED CHILD

What happens in the mind, the body, and the life of a child who grows up inside alienation

12. Looking at the Child

There are moments when a parent looks at their child and senses that something has changed, but cannot say precisely what. It is not an episode. It is not a sentence. It is a sensation that precedes thought. The gaze no longer meets yours the same way. The body seems to hold itself back. The gestures grow more cautious, the presence less spontaneous.

It is not open rejection. It is a change in the quality of the bond. In the early stages of the alienating process, the child does not yet reject openly. They are not angry, not hostile. They are confused. They sense that something is shifting in the emotional atmosphere around them, but they have no words to understand it. Very early, they learn to watch the parent they depend on, to catch subtle signals: when a topic becomes dangerous, when a feeling is welcomed and when it is pushed away.

Without anyone asking, the child begins to regulate themselves. They say less. They ask less. They hide what they feel. Not because they do not feel, but because they are learning that expressing everything they feel can put the bond at risk.

In this phase, the child internalizes a silent and immensely powerful lesson: not everything I feel is safe to say. It is not a conscious choice. It is an early adaptation, oriented toward relational survival.

From the Signals to the Process: A Reading from the Child's Point of View

The twenty signals of alienation described in Part I identify manifestations observable from the outside: attitudes, behaviors, relational patterns that allow an alienating configuration to be recognized.

The five adaptive configurations described in the next chapter make a different move: they do not answer the question "what do we observe from the outside?" but its complement: "what happens inside the child while those signals take shape?"

They do not indicate a rigid or obligatory sequence. They represent recurring configurations through which the child tries to make bearable a relational conditioning that exceeds their developmental resources.

As Fidler and Bala (2010) have shown, a child's resistance to contact cannot be understood without analyzing the relational context in which it develops: what looks from the outside like rejection, coldness, or choice is often, from the inside, the result of a defensive organization oriented toward emotional survival.

In Brief. Before the words, the quality of the bond changes: the child learns to watch the adult, to say less, to hide what they feel. The silent lesson they internalize — not everything I feel is safe to say — is the beginning of the adaptation.

13. The Five Adaptive Configurations of the Alienated Child

1. The Campaign of Rejection

In the alienated child, rejection is not born as a sudden act. It is the outcome of a gradual path. In an early phase it may show itself through avoidance, somatic symptoms, anticipatory anxiety, or unexplained irritability. Progressively, the position hardens until it becomes global and identity-based.

The child does not yet say "I don't want to see you anymore." They say instead: "I can't today," "I feel weird," "It makes me anxious." Over time, the distance consolidates. The language changes. The position stiffens. The child stops speaking in emotional terms and begins speaking in identity terms: "I don't want to see him anymore," "She's not part of my life." The rejection becomes a radical solution to an unbearable emotional conflict.

Eliminating one parent from the inner scene becomes the fastest way to switch off the tension between two loyalties, the fear of losing the other parent, the guilt of loving both. The child does not reject because they do not love. They reject because loving both has become too costly. A child says: "If I see him, I feel terrible for days afterward." They are not talking about the parent. They are talking about the conflict they cannot hold.

Over time, this configuration teaches a brutal lesson: complex bonds are not worked through — they are erased. As an adult, this child may struggle to tolerate relational conflict and tend to resolve it through clean breaks. Baker (2007) documented how, in structured cases, the rejection shows pervasive characteristics disproportionate to the excluded parent's actual behavior. Warshak (2010) notes that the absence of ambivalence and the weak justification of the rejection are distinguishing indicators relative to ordinary conflict. Childress (2015), in his clinical formulation of pathological alignment, describes the rejection as the outcome of a dysfunctional triangulation in which the child is placed in an allied, fused position with the alienating parent. The rejection is not born of an absence of love, but of the impossibility of tolerating the tension between two primary bonds.

2. Rationalization

Once the rejection takes shape, the mind needs to make it coherent. It is not enough to pull away: one must explain why. The child begins to construct reasons that justify the distance. These explanations can appear surprisingly mature, articulate, logical. But they are not born to clarify. They are born to contain. Rationalization makes it possible to move from the emotional plane to the cognitive plane. Feeling is replaced by thinking.

The pain is translated into argument: "He's not good for me." "It's toxic." "I've thought it through." "It's my choice."

It is not falsehood. It is defense. The child is not seeking historical truth. They are seeking a version that lets them stand without trembling. The parent asks: "But what did I do that was so terrible?" The child answers with a list of reasons, all apparently sensible. But while speaking, they feel nothing. The voice is steady. The body is rigid. The rationalization does not serve to communicate. It serves not to feel. Over time, this mode can become stable: the adult who emerges from it explains a great deal, feels little, and struggles to recognize their own emotions except when they become somatic.

Rationalization allows anguish to be converted into argument. Warshak (2010) observes that in alienation cases the child may present explanations surprisingly articulate for their developmental age. This is not early maturity, but a defensive process. From a psychodynamic standpoint, Vaillant (1992) describes rationalization as a defense mechanism that maintains a coherent self-image by reducing the emotional impact of conflict. Its function is not to establish truth, but to maintain internal stability.

3. Splitting

The loyalty conflict is one of the most destabilizing emotional experiences for a child. Holding together love for two warring parents requires an integrative capacity that often exceeds the developmental resources available.

When the ambivalence becomes unbearable, the mind looks for a shortcut: splitting. One parent is progressively idealized, the other progressively devalued. Not because reality is that simple, but because simplicity reduces anguish. If one is good and the other is bad, I no longer have to doubt. I no longer have to swing back and forth. I no longer have to feel guilt. Splitting protects against internal disorganization, but at an enormous cost: it eliminates complexity, impoverishes feeling, and stiffens identity. Kernberg (1975) described splitting as a primitive defense mechanism that prevents the integration of contradictory representations of the object; in the alienated child, this mechanism is activated and maintained by external relational pressure.

"He's always been like that." "She never understood anything." The sentences are absolute. Without nuance. Not because the child has become rigid, but because rigidity protects them from collapse.

In ordinary conflict, the child maintains complex representations. In structured alienation, complexity is eliminated. Fonagy et al. (2002) link splitting to impaired mentalization: when the relational system is highly stressful, the capacity to integrate contradictory mental states shrinks. Childress (2015) interprets splitting in the alienating context as the result of a transgenerational transmission of disorganized attachment patterns. Splitting protects against internal chaos, but it stiffens identity.

4. Identification

As the process advances, the child no longer merely rejects one parent. They begin to resemble the other more and more. In language, in tone, in gestures, in posture, in convictions. This is not conscious imitation.

It is a process of deep identification. Becoming similar is a way of belonging. And belonging, in that context, is a matter of safety. The implicit message: "If I am like you, I won't lose you." The targeted parent hears the child repeat the same sentences, in the same tone, with the same linguistic structure as the other parent. It is not provocation. It is identity alignment.

Over time, this identification can obstruct the process of individuation. The child grows, but remains tied to an identity built more for protection than for authenticity.

This phenomenon can be read in light of Minuchin's systemic theories (1974), which describe how, in enmeshed family systems, generational boundaries are compromised. Garber (2020) speaks of dyadic enmeshment, in which the child becomes the parent's emotional regulator. From the attachment standpoint, Bowlby (1969) notes that the need for proximity and safety can prevail over individual authenticity when the system perceives threat. If Bowlby provided the theoretical frame, it is Mary Ainsworth who made it observable. With the Strange Situation paradigm, Ainsworth (1978) translated attachment into recognizable patterns: secure, insecure-avoidant, insecure-ambivalent, to which Main and Solomon (1990) would later add the disorganized pattern. This grid is decisive for reading alienation. The child who aligns with the alienating parent is not choosing affection: they are seeking a secure base in a relational field that has been made unstable for them. When the figure who should reassure is also the source of the tension, the child has no coherent strategy available, and organizes their security around the one bond they perceive as non-negotiable. Identification is not imitation. It is a strategy of belonging.

5. Emotional Anesthesia

The last passage is perhaps the deepest. When the conflict lasts long, when the splitting hardens, the emotional system performs one further reduction: it stops feeling.

Not completely, not everywhere — selectively. Empathy toward the rejected parent switches off. Longing is anesthetized. Tenderness becomes a risk. The child can appear cold, distant, indifferent. They are not. They are protecting an equilibrium built at great cost. "I don't feel anything." "It's over for me." They say it without anger. Without visible pain. Emotional anesthesia is not healing. It is suspension.

Emotional complexity — the coexistence of positive and negative aspects — becomes unbearable. Events that might favor a revision of the narrative do not produce integration: they are devalued, denied, or reinterpreted to confirm the initial position. Professionals and institutions are delegitimized when they fail to confirm the dominant narrative. Fonagy (2002) links the reduction of mentalizing capacity to coercive, highly conflictual relational contexts.

In Brief. Five adaptive configurations: the campaign of rejection, rationalization, splitting, identification, emotional anesthesia. They are not choices and they are not malice: they are how a mind still in formation stays standing inside a conflict that exceeds it.

14. Variations by Age, Gender, and Position Among Siblings

How the Dynamic Changes Shape Over Time

The alienating dynamic keeps the same core at every stage of growth. What changes is the form it takes: the language, the quality of the withdrawal, the kind of defense that mind and body manage to organize with the developmental resources available. The ages are not rigid compartments, but prevailing configurations.

The Young Child (Ages 4–8)

At this stage the rejection is rarely structured or verbalized. It expresses itself mainly through the body: resistance to visits without being able to explain why, crying or stiffening before transitions, somatic symptoms, regressions.

The mind does not yet have the cognitive tools to build a coherent narrative; what dominates is the need for safety. The child does not consciously choose a parent: they anchor themselves to whatever they perceive as indispensable to emotional stability. If the dynamic persists, separation anxiety can become chronic, and the body becomes the main site where the distress is expressed.

Attachment research shows that when a significant figure becomes simultaneously a source of comfort and of tension, the nervous system privileges relational survival over emotional coherence (Main & Solomon, 1990; Schore, 2003).

The Preteen (Ages 9–12)

The rejection begins to find words, but it is not yet fully structured: "I don't feel like it," "He bothers me," "I'm not comfortable." The tone is defensive more than accusatory. At this stage identity is under construction; rejection can become a way of reducing an internal conflict perceived as unmanageable.

If the dynamic consolidates, the capacity for doubt tends to narrow and thinking becomes progressively more polarized. The rejection can pass from a vaguely defined discomfort to an organized relational position, sustained by a relatively coherent narrative. In this age range the child has more language, more episodic memory, and more capacity for argument: this is why the alienating dynamic tends to show itself less as "silence" and more as rationalization.

1) Trigger: loyalty becomes a safety strategy. The process often activates when the child perceives that the relationship with one parent "endangers" the equilibrium with the other. Explicit coercion is not always needed: a repeated climate of disapproval, tension, or vulnerability in the preferred parent can be enough to induce the child to reduce ambivalence in order to maintain belonging and stability (Kelly & Johnston, 2001; Johnston, Walters & Olesen, 2005). At this stage the sentences are still "defensive," but they begin to become positional: "He makes me anxious," "It's not good for me," "I don't want to go anymore."

2) The narrative begins: reasons that are weak but "certain." Between ages 9 and 12 the likelihood increases that the child will produce explanations — often, however, disproportionate, vague, not anchored to verifiable episodes, or repetitive. Kelly and Johnston describe the passage from simple rejection to a configuration in which the child tends to idealize one parent and devalue the other, with a narrowing of doubt (Kelly & Johnston, 2001). Here the typical signals appear: "small" reasons justifying a "total" decision, global rejection of the parent.

3) Maintenance: relational reinforcements and closure to corrective experiences. The alienating process tends to maintain itself through multiple reinforcements: relief from loyalty anxiety, approval and attention from the preferred parent, reduction of dissonance ("if I reject him, then he must deserve it"). The contemporary literature on post-separation rejection insists on a differential and multifactorial approach: the alienated condition should be read as the outcome of an interaction among the child's vulnerabilities, parenting styles, conflict, and communication patterns, not as a single isolated act (Fidler, Bala & Saini, 2013; Saini, Johnston, Fidler & Bala, 2016). In preadolescence, when the position crystallizes, the "door" that most often closes is the door of doubt: the child becomes progressively impervious to positive memories, contrary evidence, and attempts at repair.

The Adolescent (Ages 13–17): Alienation as Identity Organization

In adolescence the rejection is no longer merely a strategy for regulating internal conflict. It can become a structured identity position. The statements take declared, argued form: "It's my choice." "He's not good for me." "I've figured out who you are."

The developmental difference is decisive: the adolescent possesses abstract thought, complex narrative construction, and moral formulation of judgment.

This makes the rejection less impulsive and more systematized. Identity risks being built "against" rather than "from." Over time, identity rigidity, polarized relationships, or difficulty integrating ambivalence and complexity may appear.

1. Developmental autonomy and relational pseudo-autonomy. Adolescence is physiologically oriented toward differentiation and the construction of the self. In contexts of persistent parental conflict, however, the need for autonomy can intertwine with alienating dynamics, turning alignment with one parent into a proof of subjective independence (Kelly & Johnston, 2001; Fidler, Bala & Saini, 2013). The adolescent may perceive the rejection as an act of self-determination, a conscious choice, a moral stand. The conviction of "thinking for myself" can be authentically felt, even when the narrative reflects a polarized relational organization. Here autonomy is not absent: it is oriented oppositionally.

2. Moralization and global judgment. Unlike in preadolescence, the rejection at this stage frequently takes on an ethical dimension. The rejected parent is not just a source of discomfort: they are defined as a person in global, stable terms. The literature describes how, in structured rejection, dispositional attributions can emerge ("that's just how he is"), generalizations extended across time, negative retrospective reinterpretations of the entire relational history, and an absence of declared ambivalence (Johnston, Walters & Olesen, 2005). The adolescent may reread even previously neutral or positive memories in light of the new identity position.

3. Behavioral radicalization. In the adolescent alienating process, the rejection does not remain merely cognitive or emotional: it becomes behavioral and organized. There may be active, stable refusal of contact, declared opposition in front of third parties, intentional communication blocking, recruitment of peers into the narrative, extension of hostility to the extended family (Fidler & Bala, 2010). In this age range, the rejection can be publicly defended, supported with coherent arguments, and maintained over time without significant oscillation.

4. Identity built "against." Adolescent identity is normally built by integrating differences and belongings. In a structured alienating dynamic, it can instead organize itself by opposition. The self is defined against a parent: against their last name, against their history, against their value system. Polarization becomes a founding element of identity. It is no longer just a way to reduce conflict: it is a declaration of who one is. Kelly and Johnston (2001) note that in these cases the rejection tends to present as a definitive choice, not a negotiable position.

5. Crystallization and imperviousness. When the process consolidates, one observes stability of the position over time, imperviousness to corrective experiences, refusal of dissonant information, strong narrative coherence. The literature on interparental conflict shows that chronic exposure to polarizing dynamics is associated with difficulties in emotional regulation and in future intimate relationships (Harold & Sellers, 2018). In an alienating context, such exposure can contribute to identity rigidity and difficulty integrating relational complexity.

Differential elements relative to ages 9–12: in adolescence the alienating process is distinguished by the ideological dimension of the rejection, the moralization of judgment, and active behavioral organization.

The Young Adult (Ages 18–25)

The rejection is rationalized: "I chose this," "It's better this way," "I don't want to reopen it." Legal adulthood does not necessarily coincide with narrative autonomy. The history may not have been reworked, but absorbed as identity. Developmental neuroscience shows that the maturation of the prefrontal cortex, implicated in critical revision and narrative integration, is completed only in young adulthood (Siegel, 2020). This means the possibility of rereading can emerge even late.

Unlike the adolescent, the young adult possesses legal, economic (sometimes partial), and decisional autonomy. At this stage the rejection is no longer impulsive or ideologically oppositional: it is often integrated into the sense of self. The family history may not have been truly reworked, but absorbed as a stable part of identity. The account appears coherent, linear, without oscillation. There is no longer any need to defend the position: it is simply "how it is."

1. Rationalization and narrative coherence. The young adult tends to explain the rejection in terms of a conscious, well-considered choice. The narrative can appear mature, reflective, detached. Yet narrative coherence does not necessarily mean critical integration. The literature on alienation in adulthood shows that many young adults exposed to alienating behaviors in childhood or adolescence report a rigidly organized family history, with difficulty tolerating alternative versions or dissonant information (Verhaar et al., 2022). At this stage the rejection is no longer active conflict: it has become structure.

2. Legal autonomy vs. psychological autonomy. The legal capacity to choose is not the same as the emotional capacity to reconsider. Many young adults maintain the position taken in adolescence not out of opposition, but out of narrative continuity: changing the version would mean calling into question a significant part of their identity. Fidler, Bala, and Saini (2013) note that the effects of alienating dynamics can persist even when the parental conflict has subsided, precisely because the narrative has been internalized.

3. Neurobiological maturation and the possibility of rereading. Developmental neuroscience indicates that maturation of the prefrontal cortex — implicated in integration, emotional regulation, critical revision, and cognitive flexibility — continues into young adulthood (Siegel, 2020). This finding has significant clinical relevance: the possibility of reconsidering one's relational history can emerge even late. It is not rare for doubts previously absent to appear between ages 20 and 25 — curiosity toward the rejected parent, revision of consolidated memories, reopening of dialogue. The plasticity is no longer as broad as in childhood, but it is not over.

4. Possible outcomes. Absent any reworking, difficulties may emerge in intimate relationships, fear of abandonment or of fusion, rigidity in handling conflict, a monolithic family narrative, vulnerability to depression or anxiety. Studies of young adults exposed to alienating behaviors show associations with greater psychological distress and relational difficulty even years later (Portilla-Saavedra et al., 2023). Yet unlike adolescence, here a new developmental movement is possible: autonomous critical revision.

5. Difference from adolescence. If in the adolescent alienation can take an ideological, oppositional form, in the young adult it tends to present as a stabilized choice, an integrated identity, a coherent narrative, an emotionally "normalized" distance. It is no longer a stand being taken: it is a closed chapter. But the closure can be apparent.

The Adult: Stabilization, Adaptation, and Functional Repression

The rejection can appear stabilized, normalized, accompanied by apparent serenity. The adult who keeps a distance from a parent may show no anger, conflict, or visible emotional activation. The position appears coherent, integrated into the biography, rarely discussed. The account is brief, linear, without manifest tension.

1. Defensive stabilization. With the passing years, what in adolescence was polarization can turn into structural adaptation. The rejection is no longer an active choice: it is a consolidated relational configuration. In some cases, defense mechanisms such as splitting or compartmentalization can remain operative even in the absence of visible conflict. The mechanism is the one described in Chapter 13: separate, unintegrated representations of the relational object, with a reduction of anguish paid for at the price of affective integration (Kernberg, 1975). In the adult, this can show as affective neutralization ("I don't care anymore"), reduced emotional memory, persistent rationalization, systematic avoidance of anything that reactivates the topic. There is no longer ideological polarization: there is internal separation.

2. Compartmentalization and adaptive functioning. Compartmentalization allows adequate functioning at work, socially, and in one's own family, while maintaining an unprocessed relational fracture. The adult can build a family of their own, stable relationships, a coherent professional identity, without the original knot necessarily being recrossed. This does not imply structural pathology. It can be an adaptive solution: but the absence of manifest conflict is not the same as complete narrative integration.

3. Reactivating events. Unlike in the young adult, here the reopening does not come from neurodevelopmental maturation but from life events: the birth of a child, a parent's illness or death, a personal relational crisis, psychotherapy. Such events can reactivate representations that had remained compartmentalized and generate a sense of unrecognized loss, late grief, unexpected internal conflict, a need for narrative revision.

4. Possible outcomes. In mature adulthood, the possible configurations vary: stable and functional rejection, partial relational reopening, reconciliation, continued distance without conflict. The central variable is not the presence or absence of contact, but the level of internal integration. An adult can maintain distance without splitting, just as they can maintain contact without integration.

One constant runs through all the ages: what changes is not the existence of the love, but the access to it. The child does not necessarily stop loving. They may learn to compartmentalize what they feel in order to preserve an equilibrium perceived as necessary. The alienating dynamic does not erase the emotional bond; it can limit its possibility of conscious expression or narrative integration.

Why Some Children Pull Away and Others Stay

Two children grow up in the same context, go through the same separation, and yet react differently. It is not a matter of strength or weakness. It is a matter of where and how the pain finds room.

Some children are especially sensitive to emotional atmospheres. They perceive subtle tensions, loaded silences, micro-shifts in the relational climate. At a certain point they make an invisible move: they withdraw. Not from an absence of love, but because the intensity becomes unbearable. Pulling away becomes a regulation strategy. Other children resist by staying. They close no doors, take no sharp positions, but live in constant balance, careful never to shift too much weight to one side. They do not break; they hold. The price is different: a silent, prolonged internal tension. Attachment theory and research on adaptive strategies show that children organize different modes in the face of the same stressful context (Crittenden, 1995). There is no strong child and fragile child. There is the child who, at that moment, found the strategy that seemed least dangerous.

When the Child Is a Boy, When the Child Is a Girl

When the child is a boy, the distance may show as progressive subtraction: fewer words, fewer explanations, less emotional contact. Not necessarily attack, but reduction. Feeling is contained through doing, thinking, rationalizing. In adulthood, this can translate into difficulty opening up in intimate relationships when vulnerability is asked of him. It is not a lack of feeling, but the bodily memory of an emotion that was once risky. When the child is a girl, the distance may take the form of involvement. The daughter may enter the story, take sides, assume functions of emotional support. Loyalty becomes identity. Over time, this can complicate psychological separation, generating conflicts between autonomy and guilt. These are not fixed or biologically determined roles, but recurring configurations observed in many clinical histories.

When the Distance Involves the Mother or the Father

When the distance involves the mother, the primary dimension of affect regulation may be touched. In many developmental histories, the mother represents the first function of emotional containment. The estrangement can foster an early defensive self-sufficiency: "I don't need her" becomes a way of protecting oneself from the pain of needing. When it involves the father, the function of recognition, limit-setting, and legitimation toward the outside world may be engaged. The absence can affect the relationship with authority, autonomy, and the sense of personal legitimacy. These are not exclusive roles: they are relational functions that can be performed by either parent. In families with several children, alienation rarely distributes evenly. The system assigns roles: one child rejects openly, one stays in hidden contact, one mediates, one withdraws. Not because of greater or lesser understanding, but because of different adaptive organization. Beneath all the variants one constant remains: adaptation precedes choice.

In Brief. The core stays, the form changes with age: the body in the young child, rationalization in the preteen, identity in the adolescent, structure in the young adult and the adult. Beneath all the variants, one constant: adaptation precedes choice.

15. The Impossible Empathy

Why the Alienated Child Struggles to Feel Empathy for the Rejected Parent

In the early phases the empathy exists: longing, tenderness, the desire to come close. But if every emotional reactivation generates tension, guilt, or fear of destabilizing the family equilibrium, the psychic system intervenes. It does not eliminate empathy globally: it redistributes it. The child can be empathic with friends, teachers, animals, yet experience a selective closure toward the rejected parent.

Not from a lack of feeling, but because that feeling has become dangerous. In terms of affect regulation, when an emotion activates relational threat, the organism tends to reduce it (Schore, 2003). To make the distance sustainable, the mind constructs a simplified narrative.

Ambivalence is reduced. One is right, the other is wrong. This polarization protects against the anguish of doubt. Splitting reduces internal complexity and stabilizes the equilibrium (Kernberg, 1975). In some configurations, the empathy is hooked to a protective role: the child perceives one parent as fragile or wounded and feels they must hold them up. In that configuration, feeling empathy for the other can be experienced as betrayal. Fonagy and colleagues (2002) described how, in insecure attachment contexts, mentalization can shrink when the relationship becomes a source of threat.

The child does not choose against a parent. They choose the configuration that allows them to maintain internal stability.

The Body of the Alienated Child

Before the words, the body changes. The gaze avoids or monitors. Facial expression narrows. Posture stiffens. Spontaneity contracts.

It is not coldness: it is containment. The autonomic nervous system registers chronic relational stress and modulates the somatic response even in the absence of conscious verbalization (van der Kolk, 2014). The body can become the place where what cannot be said gets expressed: recurrent stomachaches, headaches, sleep disturbances, muscle tension. Sometimes a growing bodily resemblance to the favored parent is observed: posture, tone, gestures.

This precedence of the body over the word finds its grounding in the neurosequential model (Perry & Szalavitz, 2017): because the lower areas of the brain, which regulate stress, mature first, chronic relational stress is registered on the somatic and neurovegetative plane before it can be thought or said. The alienated child's bodily symptom is thus not an epiphenomenon, but the language of the system that was structured first.

It is not superficial imitation, but embodied belonging. The voice can become flat or surprisingly adult. Play diminishes. The body takes up less space or, on the contrary, stiffens into excessive control. These are different modes of the same strategy: keeping balance in a context perceived as unstable.

As an adult, someone who grew up in such configurations may have difficulty recognizing their own emotions, or experience intimacy as an excessive demand. Not from structural incapacity, but because the body learned early that feeling too much could destabilize the system. The body of the alienated child is not a body without emotion. It is a body that learned to regulate emotional expression in the service of safety.

In Brief. The alienated child's empathy does not disappear: it is redistributed, because toward the rejected parent it has become dangerous. And the body speaks before the words: gaze, posture, somatic symptoms. It is not coldness: it is containment.

16. Digital Control and the Point of No Return

When the Phone Becomes a Management Tool

Contemporary alienation is not played out only in words spoken face to face. The cell phone allows the alienating parent to keep constant contact with the child even when the child is physically with the other parent.

The messages can be frequent, apparently caring — "Everything okay?", "Text me as soon as you get there," "Tell me what you're doing" — but in the alienating process they become instruments of monitoring. The child is kept permanently connected. There is no truly separate space in which they can live the experience with the other parent unobserved.

Sometimes the control is more explicit: details, information, reports are requested. The child learns that reporting back is not optional. The alienating parent may suggest keeping the phone on, not deleting messages, sending screenshots. Not always in a threatening tone — often with the justification of protection: "It's for safety," "That way I know you're okay."

The implicit message is powerful: I protect you, but to do it I need you to be my eyes.

The child learns to regulate themselves in advance: they avoid situations that might generate questions, trim stories that might create tension, select what they communicate. It is not only manipulation: it is a system of relational dependence mediated by technology. And the more subtle and everyday the control, the more normal it becomes. The phone is not the problem: it is the means through which the pressure is maintained.

Autonomy is not forbidden. It simply has no room to develop. The literature on coercive control in intimate relationships shows how constant surveillance, even when disguised as care or protection, can progressively limit the other's psychological autonomy, turning the bond into a space of monitoring rather than trust (Stark, 2007).

The Point of No Return

There are moments, in alienation histories, when something changes definitively. It is the moment the child is drawn into a story that turns the rejected parent from a distant or painful figure into a threat. The distance stops being emotional and becomes moral. Often, that is where the bond breaks in a nearly irreversible way.

To accuse means redefining one's entire history. It means looking back and saying that what was, was not what it seemed; that what made you feel safe was actually dangerous; that the love you felt was a mistake. In that passage, the child is not only talking about a parent: they are rewriting themselves.

When a child is pushed, directly or indirectly, to recount abuse, they cross a threshold from which it is hard to return. That account becomes a refuge: a new house to live in so as not to feel the chaos. Repeating that story gives order, switches off the doubt. If the rejected parent is guilty, the splitting is justified. If he is dangerous, the absence of empathy is necessary.

Often, after this passage, the relationship is interrupted from the outside as well: contact halted, visits suspended, institutionalized silence. For the child, this is powerful confirmation. If the adults intervene, then what was said must be true. With time, shame sets in: going back would mean admitting to having accused unjustly. For many children, this is an intolerable weight. Not because the love is missing, but because the psychic cost of reconsidering is too high.

From that moment, the splitting changes quality. It is no longer an emotional division: it becomes a moral division. There is no more room for nuance. Everything is rewritten in the light of a single truth. And that truth, even when it hurts, holds things together.

To say this is not to deny the existence of real abuse, which exists and must always be recognized, addressed, and protected against. It is to distinguish. Because when a child is led to recount something they did not live as their own experience, they do not lose only a parent. They lose the possibility of a complex story, the right to ambivalence, the road to a possible return.

Here, more than anywhere else, the fate of the bond is decided.

In Brief. The phone enables continuous control disguised as care: the child no longer has a separate space in which to live the other parent. The point of no return comes when distance becomes accusation: from there, going back means rewriting oneself.

17. What Not to Do with a Child in an Alienated Configuration

When a child is in an alienated configuration, the most frequent — and most understandable — error is to treat them as if they were free to choose. Many interventions fail because they start from a mistaken premise: the idea that the child is asserting an autonomous will, when in reality they are trying to protect a fragile internal equilibrium.

This chapter is not written to blame the rejected parent. It is written to avoid the moves that, however human, end up reinforcing the alienating configuration.

Do not ask them to choose. Saying "You know how things really went" sounds respectful. In reality it exposes the child to a responsibility they cannot bear. In an alienated configuration, the choice is not free. Asking them to choose reactivates the loyalty conflict: any answer will put a bond at risk. The father says: "Tell me what you want to do. I'll respect your choice." The child lowers their eyes and answers: "Then I don't want to see you." Inside, though, they do not feel they have chosen. They only feel that, had they said anything else, something fundamental would have been lost.

Do not argue against their narrative. Responding with "That's not true," "That's not how it happened" — even when you are certain of its unreliability — produces the opposite effect. The child's narrative is not just an account of facts: it has become identity. Questioning it amounts to threatening their internal stability. The more you contradict it, the more the narrative hardens.

Do not defend yourself by over-explaining. Detailed justifications, painstaking reconstructions are experienced as pressure, not help. The child is not looking for clarification: they are looking for safety. The parent tries to explain, point by point. The child listens in silence, then says: "See? You always talk about yourself." Not because they did not understand, but because hearing you explain puts them under pressure.

Do not ask them for empathy. Saying "Think about how I feel," "Can't you see you're hurting me?" asks for something the child, at this moment, cannot give. To feel empathy they would have to reactivate guilt, ambivalence, conflict — everything their system is avoiding. The result is not opening; it is closure.

Do not use the truth as a weapon. Phrases like "One day you'll understand," "The truth will come out" do not reassure. The child feels a silent pressure, as if sooner or later they will have to prove they chose the right side. It does not reassure them: it stiffens them.

Do not expect gratitude or recognition. Recognizing your pain would mean questioning the narrative that keeps them in balance. The expectation of recognition generates frustration and new ruptures.

Do not react with rage or despair in front of them. Intense emotions become confirmation of relational danger. The child reinforces emotional control and detachment.

Do not force the timeline. Every acceleration produces hardening. Do not demand immediate clarifications, decisions, rapid changes.

Not doing these things does not mean giving up. It means not making the structure worse. With a child in an alienated configuration, the first treatment is not doing more. It is stopping what reinforces the cage. Only when the pressure decreases does it become possible, over time, for something to move.

> **In Brief.** With a child in an alienated configuration, the error is treating them as if they were free. Do not ask them to choose, do not argue against their narrative, do not ask them for empathy, do not use the truth as a weapon, do not force the timeline. The first treatment is to stop doing what reinforces the cage.

PART V — VOICES OF CHILDREN

18. Voices of Children and What Remains

The names, places, and identifying details in the accounts that follow have been changed to protect the privacy of those involved. Any resemblance to real persons, specific events, or particular court proceedings is purely coincidental and unintentional.

Four Accounts

The stories that follow come from direct interviews conducted by the author with children who grew up in contexts of parental alienation. They have no evidentiary value. They serve to show what happens in a child's mind when they grow up inside a dynamic they cannot name.

1. Silent Alienation and the Possible Return

Marco says there was no precise moment when he stopped seeing his father. There was a slow slide, the way something becomes too heavy to carry and the body, before the mind, finds a way out. His father appeared fragile — not openly, but in that subtle form a child picks up immediately: hesitations, implicit requests, a suffering that seemed to ask for protection.

His mother, by contrast, appeared strong, centered, able to hold. For a child, this asymmetry weighs more than any words. Marco says he never thought he had to choose. He found himself, without realizing it, in the role of defender. Protecting whoever appears fragile becomes natural, almost inevitable. And when a child takes on this role, going back becomes difficult. Not only out of loyalty, but out of shame: questioning that loyalty would mean admitting to having supported something destructive. Going back means betraying not only a parent, but the version of yourself you built in order to survive.

For years he told his story coherently, linearly, without hesitation. But over time that coherence began to weigh on him. Not as sudden doubt, but as tiredness — a deep, wordless tiredness. It was only when the relational pressure eased, when no one demanded coherence or allegiance anymore, that something reopened. Not immediate forgiveness, not an easy reconciliation, but an internal space that was less threatening.

The return was not a sudden act of courage: it was the result of an internal security that, finally, no longer depended on protecting someone. Marco felt, for the first time, an emptiness. Not longing. Emptiness. And into that emptiness a question crept: "What if it isn't all that simple?"

The return was not an embrace. It was a short text message. Then a coffee. Then a shared silence with no need for explanations. It did not erase the past. It only reopened a space in which doubt was no longer dangerous.

It was internal security finally sufficient to tolerate ambivalence.

2. When the Body Interrupts the Loyalty

A young woman recounts that for years she maintained a narrative she did not truly feel as her own, but which let her keep her balance. It was a story that explained the world, that gave meaning to the pain, that made the distance bearable. She never felt manipulated: she felt responsible. Responsible for not letting a parent who cried often collapse, for not adding pain to a pain already too great.

Every time she felt longing for the other parent, something closed in her stomach. It was not a voice scolding her. It was a physical tension. At twenty, the symptoms began: persistent insomnia, sudden tachycardia, an exhaustion no vacation resolved.

The body began to say no before the mind was ready. And when physical survival becomes the priority, loyalty loses force. Not by moral choice, but by limit. She started therapy for anxiety. She did not talk about alienation. She talked about exhaustion. The body had begun to say no before the mind was ready to revise the story.

The turning point was not a recovered memory. It was a physical collapse. "I can't hold it all up anymore," she said one day. And in that sentence was everything: the loyalty, the fear, the responsibility that was never hers.

In this story there is no serene reworking: there is a necessary detachment. The truth does not arrive as a liberating revelation, but as a boundary. Not everything can be integrated; not everything can be repaired. Sometimes the most a child can do is stop hurting themselves. And this, even when it looks like coldness from the outside, is a form of survival.

3. The Truth That Does Not Mend

Two adults recount having recognized that a narrative was not a genuinely lived experience, but the product of powerful relational pressures. They describe the struggle of accepting that they contributed, without meaning to, to a grave miscarriage of justice. They describe the shame, the guilt, the pain.

And yet the story does not close with a mending. Understanding does not always save. Some wounds pass the threshold of the repairable. Promising what is not always possible is another form of violence. In Baker's retrospective study (2007), conducted with forty adult children, 38.5 percent of those who had recognized the alienation they suffered in childhood had not managed to fully reestablish the relationship with the excluded parent.

What runs through all these stories is not weakness, but a strength built too early and at too high a price. These are children who internalized the idea that they had to save themselves. Behind their lucidity there is almost always a silent grief: the grief for a childhood that was not protected.

4. The Invisible Loyalty

Elena was eight when she began avoiding telling what she did on weekends. There had been no explicit prohibition. There had been a change in tone. Every time she mentioned her father, her mother went silent. She said nothing bad. But she closed up. Elena learned to talk less. To report less. To select. It was not a conscious choice. It was relational learning.

At twelve she began saying her father was "shallow." At fifteen she called him "selfish." The words were hers, but the structure of the judgment was not entirely. At eighteen she cut off the relationship completely. There had been no grave event. Only an accumulation of tensions and the conviction that "it was better this way."

Years later, in therapy for relational difficulties, she noticed a detail: every time someone came emotionally close, she found a reason to push them away. "He's selfish." "He's not reliable." "He's not enough."

The words were the same ones she had used for her father. She did not go back to him. She did not feel she could. But she understood that her rigidity had not been born from an isolated fact. It was an old adaptation.

Invisible loyalty does not always show itself as attack. Sometimes it shows itself as a repeated relational pattern.

In Brief. Four stories, four paths: the return made possible by easing pressure, the body that interrupts the loyalty, the truth that does not mend, the invisible loyalty repeated in adult relationships. Behind these children's lucidity there is almost always a grief: the grief for an unprotected childhood.

19. When Lying Becomes Survival

Two Accounts, Two Paths, One Wound

This book has described parental alienation through theory, clinical work, and case law. It has analyzed the dynamics, the adaptive configurations, the mechanisms of manipulation, the system's errors, the false accusations. It has tried to give a language to what too often has none.

But there is a level of knowledge that no grid, no bibliography, and no protocol can replace: the voice of someone who lived the process from the inside. Not as a parent. Not as a professional. As a child.

The two accounts that follow were gathered by the author through direct interviews with now-adult children who chose to tell their experience. Both interviews are publicly available online.

Why two cases. The choice to present two accounts rather than one answers a scientific need and an ethical principle. The scientific need: parental alienation has no single profile. There is no single type of alienating parent, no single type of alienated child, no single level of severity, no single path out.

The two cases selected present structurally different configurations, and reading them side by side allows us to observe how the same fundamental dynamics, described in Chapter 4, can manifest in radically different forms, producing harm of different kinds and intensities.

The ethical principle: parental alienation is not a gendered phenomenon. Chapter 2 identifies the gender error among the five most frequent diagnostic errors — the automatic assumption that the alienating parent is the mother or that the targeted parent is the father. The international research (Harman et al., 2018; Harman & Matthewson, 2020) documents that either parent can be the agent or the target of the alienating dynamic.

Presenting one case in which the alienating parent is the mother and one in which the alienating parent is the father is not rhetorical balancing: it is the operational translation of a scientific finding. This book does not take the side of a gender. It takes the side of the children.

Two configurations. The first case presents the extreme form of alienation. Two brothers, now adults, were drawn as minors into a process that culminated in the construction of false accusations of sexual abuse against their father. The accusations were maintained in court for years. The father was convicted and later exonerated on review. The children, now adults, have publicly declared the accusations unfounded and described the conditioning process they were subjected to. The mother is the alienating figure. The level of severity corresponds to the extreme configuration described in Chapter 10.

The second case presents the form most frequently encountered in clinical practice and most often missed: silent alienation. A son, now an adult, reports having lived through a process of estrangement from his mother during childhood and adolescence, conducted by his father through guilt, role reversal, and daily devaluation. No court, no false accusation, no criminal proceeding. Only a slow work of erosion of the bond. The father is the alienating figure. The severity corresponds to the moderate-to-severe configuration.

What they show together. Read separately, each case illustrates a path. Read together, the two cases show something broader.

They show that alienation can be violent or silent, explicit or subterranean, accompanied by false accusations or devoid of any dramatic event — and that in both cases the harm to the child is real, deep, and lasting.

The first son describes physical terror, the performance in front of judges, the recantation ignored. The second describes the guilt, the elimination of his mother from his own mind, emotional anesthesia as a survival strategy. Different forms. The same wound: the loss of the right to love freely.

They show that the way out of alienation can come by different routes. In the first case, the awakening is triggered by a third-party professional — a group-home youth counselor — and confirmed by direct contact with the father. In the second, the exit is autonomous: it is born from disappointment with the alienating parent and from the encounter with a relationship between equals. In both cases, the process takes time; and in both cases the damage does not end with the reunion.

They show, finally, a fact that runs through this entire book: the voice of the alienated child, while still inside the process, is not a free voice. It is a voice that obeys invisible rules, that repeats constructed narratives, that defends positions not its own.

But when the pressure eases — through outside intervention, through internal evolution, through the simple passage of time — that same voice can become the most lucid and most honest document of what happened. The accounts that follow are that document.

Methodological Note

The interviews were conducted by the author with adults who have made their experience public. The contents are reported in reworked and analyzed form, not as a full transcript.

The interviewees' statements constitute personal, subjective testimony. The analysis accompanying each case is phenomenological in character: it identifies correspondences between the statements made and the dynamics described in this book's theoretical model, without constituting a determination of the facts reported.

In the first case an external judicial corroboration is available (exoneration on review). In the second case the testimony is unilateral, and the other parent's perspective is not available. This difference is declared and kept in view in the analysis.

Names, identifying references, and details that could allow recognition of the subjects or their family members have been omitted. Direct quotations, set in italics, are taken from the public interviews and attributed by family role, not by personal identity.

The analyses in the chapters that follow serve exclusively scientific and educational purposes. They do not constitute an expert opinion, do not replace individualized clinical or forensic evaluation, and are not usable as evidence in court without appropriate specialized technical assessment.

The scientific interest of the statements reported lies in the retrospective analysis of how the account was formed and in the description of the family dynamic by someone who lived it.

Before any theory of parental alienation, there is a datum no manual can replace: the voice of the children. Not the voice collected in an evaluator's office, where the context is already institutional and the words are already filtered. The voice that emerges afterward, when the pressure eases and the mind can finally reexamine what it lived.

The interview that follows allows us to observe from the inside the process described in the preceding parts of this book.

Before the Fracture

The starting point is a healthy bond. The memory that precedes the manipulation is not ambiguous. The older brother recounts: *"To me my dad was a friend — there was a friendship that was practically infinite. We went fishing together, he taught me everything I know... about radios, electronics, video games. There was a beautiful relationship; he never let us go without his time or his affection."*

No ambivalence, fear, or discomfort emerges. The bond is described with the sensory specificity of authentic memories: the fishing, the electronics, the video games. It is not an abstract reconstruction. It is embodied memory. This datum establishes a baseline: the rejection that will follow has no roots in the son's direct experience of his father. Its roots are elsewhere.

The Awareness of the Lie

The most significant passage of the entire interview concerns the relationship between what the brothers knew and what they said. The older brother states: *"In my specific case, I knew I was lying about being a victim. But my mother somehow managed to convince me that my father had hurt some other child... I knew he had done nothing to me and my brother, but my mother told me that an evaluation had found my cousin was a victim. I trusted her and I believed her word... I hated myself for what I was saying, but I kept wondering whether he really had hurt the others."*

Here we observe the fracture between personal memory and induced reality (Ceci & Bruck, 1995; Loftus, 1997). The child does not deny his own experience. He knows it. But he is destabilized by the introduction of supposed external evidence that creates a short circuit: direct memory says one thing, the affective authority says the opposite. The doubt is not born from the memory. It is born from the trust.

The dominant parental figure does not merely devalue the father: she repositions him as a danger to other children, transforming emotional doubt into moral doubt.

The Climate of Fear and Survival

The manipulation is not only narrative. It is environmental. The older brother describes the context: *"She used violence and psychological pressure. One technique was the look: she would come close and glare at us, because she had beaten us before. A look or the tone of her voice was enough for us to know which way to look and what we were supposed to say."*

And again: *"We had to do it to survive. I was genuinely afraid for my life. She liked everyone to see her words confirmed through us. She would persuade us to say those things and then reward us if we showed contempt for our father. To survive physically in that house, you had to say what she wanted."*

A coercive system combining physical violence, psychological pressure, and selective reinforcement. The child complies to regulate fear: the loyalty is not negotiated, it is imposed by threat. Affection is granted as a reward for rejecting the father.

The Borrowed Language

"Yes, we used terms like 'sexual violence' that the adults kept repeating to us. We didn't know what sex meant, but we repeated those words because they were put in our mouths. We were like tape recorders playing back what she wanted the judges to hear."

The image of the tape recorder is clinically exact: technical, legal, sexual concepts repeated without semantic comprehension. Warshak (2010) identifies this phenomenon as a reliable indicator of parental programming.

The Independent Thinker

The younger brother: *"Absolutely. I would say: 'I'm the one saying these things, I saw them myself.' But it's an illusion. Everything that reaches you as information from the alienating parent feels genuine to you, because she is the only reference figure you have at that moment."*

The child claims autonomy while immersed in total dependence.

The Absence of Ambivalence and of Guilt

"That's exactly how it is. The rejected parent becomes 'all wrong.' Nothing good exists. The other parent is always justified instead, even when their behavior is objectively problematic."

"We felt no guilt when we spoke badly of our father or humiliated him in front of others. Not because we had no conscience, but because we were convinced we were doing it to survive, to protect our mother."

The Extension to the Extended Family

"That happened too. The rejection wasn't only about our father, but his whole family world. Once you enter this dynamic, the exclusion becomes total."

The excluded parent's entire relational world is erased wholesale.

The Recantation Ignored

"During the recorded evidentiary interview, which lasted almost two hours, I was in front of the camera with the psychologist. At a certain point I burst into tears and said: 'Nothing I've told you is true.' She turned off the camera... but that signal of mine was not taken into consideration at all."

A minor recants in a protected setting, before a professional, with the camera on. The camera is turned off. The signal is not recorded, not assessed, not transmitted to the judge.

It is the operational confirmation of what Chapter 26 describes as a structural risk in interviewing children, and what Chapter 27 analyzes in the context of custody evaluations: when the child's voice does not confirm the prevailing hypothesis, the system tends not to see it.

The Awakening

"What changed me was the day a youth counselor at the group home told me: 'Look, your mother isn't right about everything — your mother makes mistakes like everyone else.' That's when I realized my mother wasn't all-powerful, that she didn't hold all the rights..."

"Seeing my father again after so many years was truly important. That's when I knew for certain it had all been a lie — seeing in him the will to fight."

When the pressure eases, when a third figure introduces doubt without threat, when direct contact breaks the induced narrative, a less threatening internal space can open. Direct contact dissolves the caricature built by the manipulation.

Map of the Dynamics Present in the Case

Extreme configuration with judicial escalation. The testimony allows seventeen of the twenty relational dynamics of Chapter 4 to be identified, in a high-coercion configuration with institutional involvement.

Dynamic 1 — Normalized daily devaluation. The father figure is progressively described as morally and emotionally inadequate, through a repeated and coherent narrative over time, until a negative internalized image stabilizes.

Dynamic 2 — One-way narrative. A single version of the facts is presented as exclusive truth. No room emerges for ambivalence or narrative integration.

Dynamic 3 — Protection that isolates. The supposed need to "protect" the children from the father legitimizes progressive isolation and the restriction of contact.

Dynamic 4 — Selective emotional withdrawal (in inverted form). Approval and affective reinforcement are granted when the children show contempt for the father; affection is conditional on alignment.

Dynamic 5 — The child as emotional support. The children serve as narrative confirmation and identity support for the dominant parent, including in court.

Dynamic 6 — Boundary confusion. The adult conflict and the accusatory strategy are transferred onto the minors, who become actors in the proceeding.

Dynamic 7 — Transformation into caricature. The father is repositioned as an entirely dangerous, morally deviant figure, with no residue of positive representation.

Dynamic 8 — Obstruction of contact. The bond with the excluded parent is interrupted in a structural, prolonged way.

Dynamic 9 — Rewriting of memory. The children's direct memory ("he never did anything to us") is destabilized by the introduction of supposed external evidence ("he hurt others").

Dynamic 10 — Forced loyalty. Loyalty is imposed through psychological pressure and environmental coercion ("you had to say what she wanted").

Dynamic 11 — Age-inappropriate language. Use of technical-legal and sexual terminology repeated without semantic comprehension ("we were like tape recorders").

Dynamic 12 — Absence of ambivalence. The excluded parent becomes "all wrong," the dominant parent "always justified."

Dynamic 13 — Extension of the rejection to the family network. The rejection extends to the father's entire relational context.

Dynamic 15 — Minimization of the excluded parent's pain. The father's suffering is denied or rendered irrelevant in the children's representational system during the proceeding.

Dynamic 16 — Systematic attribution of negative intentions. The father is repositioned as intentionally dangerous to other children.

Dynamic 17 — The illusion of choice. The children claim autonomy ("I'm the one saying these things"), but the autonomy is immersed in total dependence.

Dynamic 18 — Exclusive emotional dependence. The dominant parent is the only valid reference figure; dissent carries emotional and physical risk.

Dynamic 20 — Loss of the right to love freely. The bond with the father is suspended not because of negative direct experience, but for relational survival.

Dynamics not observable or not documentable in the case: Dynamic 14 and Dynamic 19 (the statements do not provide sufficient elements to include them with methodological rigor).

The Adaptive Configurations

In this case all five adaptive configurations of Chapter 13 are observable in full form. Campaign of rejection: an identity position publicly maintained in court for years, with narrative rigidity and coherent performance. Rationalization: construction of apparently autonomous reasons to sustain accusations and rejection. Splitting: complete polarization of the representational system — one parent totally negative, the other totally legitimized. Identification: assumption of the role of protectors and spokespersons of the dominant parent, including before judges and evaluators. Emotional anesthesia: the affective bond is suspended.

The Indicators of False Accusation

Progressive construction of the accusation. Active involvement of the minor as spokesperson. Use of emotionally loaded language without semantic comprehension. Narrative rigidity devoid of ambivalence. Absence of independent objective corroboration. Inability to integrate dissonant elements (the recantation ignored by the system).

The Clinical Meaning of the Testimony

This testimony does not prove a thesis. It allows us to observe from the inside a process the book describes from the outside. The children did not merely repeat suggested sentences: they constructed a coherent, detailed, emotionally sustained narrative. The memory was not invented: it was progressively shaped (Ceci & Bruck, 1995). In the alienating context, adherence is not only cognitive: it is affective and identity-based.

The confidence with which a child gives an account is not proof of factual truth. Subjective conviction can coexist with a contaminated memory. And when the alienating context loses force, an autonomous reworking of memory can emerge — a process that involves identity redefinition and the reconstruction of one's own history. Not all children manage it. Not all have the chance.

This testimony authorizes neither generalizations nor automatic suspicion of abuse reports. It imposes a methodological principle: in contexts of high conflict and possible alienation, children's testimony must be collected with structured, non-suggestive protocols, and with full awareness of the plasticity of developing memory.

Because a child can be sincerely convinced of what they say — and still not have lived what they recount.

In Brief. The extreme case: false accusations built with fear and reinforcement, children "like tape recorders," a recantation ignored by the system, the conviction of an innocent man and his exoneration on review. The confidence with which a child speaks is not proof of truth: it is often proof of the conditioning.

20. The Child Who Frees Himself Alone

The following analysis is based on the testimony of a son, now an adult, who reports having lived through a process of alienation from his mother during childhood and adolescence. The interview was conducted by the author and is publicly available online. The other parent's perspective is not available. For the criteria of analysis and confidentiality protections, see the Methodological Note in Chapter 19.

If the previous case shows alienation in its extreme form — false accusations, criminal proceedings, total exclusion — this second testimony shows the form that most often escapes recognition: silent alienation. No court. No formal accusation. No dramatic event. Only a slow, daily work of erosion of the bond between a child and a parent, conducted through guilt, tears, role reversal, and the rewriting of reality.

The son interviewed reports living through his parents' separation in childhood. In his reconstruction, his father could not tolerate the end of the marriage and transferred onto his son his own need for alliance. The alienation of the mother did not happen through violence or explicit imposition, but through a subtler mechanism that is harder to recognize: displayed fragility.

Fragility as an Instrument

The son describes his father as a figure who constantly presented himself as weak, suffering, in need of protection: *"He would tell me that Mom had a lover and that he was alone, and that if I left him I would be approving of Mom's new life and he would be alone and abandoned."*

And again: *"He said it crying, and I felt guilty and hurt for him, and obliged to console and protect him."*

The boundary between adult and child breaks: the parent leans on the child, the child becomes the consoler. But it is also a particularly insidious form of forced loyalty: the loyalty is imposed not with threat, but with guilt. Abandonment is presented not as the consequence of disobedience, but as the betrayal of a suffering person. The emotional cost of dissent is not anger: it is guilt.

Chapter 9 describes how separation is experienced by the alienating parent not as a relational event but as a wound to identity. The defensive reaction that follows — rage, resentment, the need for redress — can take different forms. In the brothers' testimony in the previous case, the reaction is violent, explicit, coercive.

Here it is subtler and, in many ways, harder to recognize: the parent does not command — he implores. He does not threaten — he weeps. The result is the same: the child is no longer free.

The Daily Devaluation

In the son's reconstruction, the father did not merely present himself as a victim: he actively constructed a negative image of the mother through repeated assertions: *"He told me lies of various kinds about my mother... besides the cheating, he said Mom mistreated me and hit me."*

"My paternal grandparents told me the same things against my mother too — I was surrounded."

The mother is progressively reduced to a negative figure — unfaithful, violent, absent — through a repeated narrative sustained by the dominant parent's entire family system. The devaluation comes not from a single voice but from a whole relational network.

The Fracture Between Knowing and Feeling

As in the previous case, the son describes a conscious dissociation between what he knows and what he feels: *"Inside, I knew none of it was true, but it was impossible for me to react — I was conditioned, psychologically subjugated."*

This sentence is the experiential confirmation of what Chapter 3 describes as the distinction between conviction and freedom: the conviction is born not from reason but from emotional necessity. The son knows the accusations against his mother are false. But the cost of acting on what he knows is too high: it would mean betraying the parent who presented himself as fragile, losing the only alliance left to him, facing an unbearable guilt.

The next passage describes a defense mechanism that Chapter 13 identifies as the fifth adaptive configuration, emotional anesthesia: *"I chose to have no contact with my mother... that way I had no guilt — so no feeling existed. I had eliminated her so I wouldn't suffer; at a certain point I no longer thought of her."*

The elimination of the mother from the mind is not an act of anger: it is an act of protection. The son cannot sustain the conflict between the emotional memory of his mother and the negative narrative surrounding her. The solution is radical: annul the bond. Stop thinking. Stop feeling. The son is not deprived of his mother by an explicit prohibition, but by a conditioning so deep that he is the one who closes the door.

Silent Alienation

The son uses an expression that deserves clinical attention: *"Mine was a silent alienation — no phone call, no message; I had simply eliminated her from my life."*

This formula describes a configuration the system struggles enormously to recognize. There is no triggering episode. There is no explicit rejection justified by accusations. There is a progressive, silent, total withdrawal. The son does not shout, does not accuse, does not report: he disappears.

For the system, a child who simply does not call his mother, does not answer messages, shows no visible distress, does not exist as an emergency. Silent alienation is the kind that reaches court latest — if it reaches court at all. And it is the kind Chapter 7 insists on when it says the system intervenes on physical danger, not on slow relational destruction.

The Autonomous Awakening

Unlike the previous case, where the awakening is triggered by a third-party professional (the group-home youth counselor), here the process is internal. The son describes two factors.

"The first was that my father ignored me — he always left me alone, devoted himself only to work, and I thought: how can this be? I did all this for you and you don't even see me? I deprived myself of my mother and you leave me alone?"

The first factor is disappointment. The parent who had asked for everything — exclusive loyalty, protection, alliance — stops being present once he has obtained what he wanted: the exclusion of the other parent. The son discovers that the need was not relational; it was instrumental. This discovery is consistent with what Chapter 10 describes as the passage from exclusive emotional dependence to the perception of the bond's instrumentality.

"The second was meeting a girl... it took me a year; I started to think... she had divorced parents, and little by little I understood that even if parents separate, it's not the children's business."

The second factor is the entry of a peer relationship — not vertical, not hierarchical, not conditional — that offers an alternative model. In a healthy relationship, the son experiences for the first time the possibility of speaking without his words carrying an emotional cost, of having an opinion without it putting a bond at risk.

It is the same principle Chapter 18 describes as the necessary condition for reworking: an internal security that no longer depends on protecting someone.

The Damage That Remains

The testimony closes with a passage no professional should ignore: *"I suffer from abandonment crises; if something negative happens I can't react right away — I feel terrible, I isolate myself, I need time to recover... I matured early, I didn't live my adolescence like other kids, and no one will give it back to me."*

The damage does not end with the reunion. The child who reenters the relationship with the targeted parent carries the structural traces of the process: abandonment anxiety, difficulty with emotional regulation, reactive isolation, lost developmental milestones. Bowlby (1973) describes how early experiences of disorganized attachment produce internal working models that reactivate in adulthood, especially in intimate relationships. The child who learned that loving is dangerous, that loyalty has a price, and that trust can be betrayed carries these schemas into future relationships. Reunion is a beginning, not a cure.

The testimony allows eleven of the twenty relational dynamics of Chapter 4 to be identified, in a non-judicial, low-institutional-visibility configuration.

Dynamic 1 (normalized daily devaluation): the mother is described through repeated, normalized assertions that progressively undermine her image ("Mom had a lover," "Mom mistreated me," "Mom hit me").

Dynamic 2 (one-way narrative): a single version of the family history is presented as the only interpretive key, with no room for complexity or rebuttal.

Dynamic 4 (selective emotional withdrawal): approval and emotional closeness are conditional on the son's alignment; the cost of dissent is associated with displayed suffering, withdrawal, or relational deprivation.

Dynamic 5 (the child as emotional support): functional role reversal — the son becomes the adult's consoler and regulator ("I felt obliged to console and protect him").

Dynamic 6 (boundary confusion): the son is drawn into the couple's conflict and called to "take sides," making it impossible to separate the marital plane from the parenting plane.

Dynamic 7 (transformation into caricature): the mother is reduced to a simplified, morally negative figure (unfaithful/violent), with loss of ambivalence and of integrated representation.

Dynamic 10 (forced loyalty): loyalty is imposed not through explicit threat but through guilt ("if I left him he would be alone and abandoned").

Dynamic 12 (absence of ambivalence): affective polarization — one parent "to be protected," the other "to be expelled," with reduced or suspended guilt toward the excluded parent.

Dynamic 13 (extension of the rejection to the family network): the devaluing narrative is reinforced by multiple figures in the same system ("my paternal grandparents told me the same things").

Dynamic 18 (exclusive emotional dependence): the dominant parent is experienced as the primary, needy reference figure, making any misalignment emotionally too costly.

Dynamic 20 (loss of the right to love freely): the son reports a radical adaptive solution: suspending the bond so as not to suffer ("I eliminated her... at a certain point I no longer thought of her").

The Adaptive Configurations

In this case three adaptive configurations are observable in full form and one in partial form.

Second configuration — Rationalization: the son constructs coherent explanations to sustain a withdrawal born of emotional constraints rather than negative direct experience ("I couldn't go back"; "it was easier to eliminate her").

Third configuration — Splitting: polarization of the representational system: the dominant parent "suffering and legitimate," the other "all wrong" and erasable.

Fifth configuration — Emotional anesthesia: selective suspension of feeling as a survival strategy ("no feeling existed... I no longer thought of her").

Fourth configuration — Identification (partial): assumption of the role of defender and protector of the dominant parent ("he needed support"), without reaching the militant, public form observable in the judicial case.

The campaign-of-rejection configuration (the first) is, by contrast, not structured in institutional or public form: the rejection expresses itself mainly as silent withdrawal and interruption of contact.

The Meaning of the Testimony

This second testimony completes the picture opened by the first. If the case of the two brothers shows alienation in its extreme form — violence, false accusations, criminal proceedings — this case shows the form most frequently encountered in clinical and forensic practice: an alienation that produces no crimes, generates no emergencies, does not arrive in court with a dramatic event. An alienation made of guilt, tears, silences — and of a child who, in order not to suffer, stops feeling.

The two cases, read together, confirm that parental alienation cuts across genders (in the first case the alienating parent is the mother, in the second the father), across levels of severity (extreme in the first, moderate-severe in the second), and across family configurations.

The son concludes with a sentence that condenses the nature of the harm: *"I was drawn into a war that was not mine."* This sentence is not a metaphor. It is the most exact definition of parental alienation from the child's point of view: a conflict between adults fought on the body, the mind, and the emotions of someone who never chose to take part in it.

What Remains in the Child, Even When They Cannot Say It

Many children who grow up inside an alienating dynamic reach adulthood carrying an invisible configuration: a difficulty tolerating ambivalence, an excessive need for control or, conversely, fusion in relationships.

They do not always speak of alienation. They speak of anxiety, of jealousy, of fear of abandonment, of an inability to trust fully. They speak of how hard it is to stay when conflict surfaces.

The adaptation does not remain confined to behavior. It organizes itself into an identity narrative. And revising that narrative is not a cognitive act: it is a restructuring of the Self.

Recantation, when it happens, is not an “I was wrong.” It is an act of enormous psychological exposure. It means accepting that what once guaranteed safety may have produced harm. Not everyone manages it. Not because intelligence is lacking. But because the internal security is not sufficient.

The alienated child is not an enemy to be convinced. They are a mind that organized itself in order not to collapse. Not all stories come back around. But all of them deserve to be understood before being judged.

The central point of this part of the book is not to establish who is right. It is to make visible the vulnerability of a mind in formation that adheres to a defensive narrative not out of malice, but because that narrative was the only way to stay standing. The alienated child is not the problem to be solved: they are the place where a relational fracture came to rest.

Asking them to choose, to understand, to come back often means asking more than they can give. Understanding this does not mean giving up the bond. It means not turning love into pressure. It means no longer asking a child to repair what they did not break.

If you are reading this as a targeted parent, these pages do not ask you to hope or to stop hoping. They ask something more concrete: do not turn your life into waiting. Your dignity does not depend on whether a child comes back. Your love is not disproven because it goes unrecognized.

In Brief. Silent alienation does not pass through the courts: it passes through guilt, tears, displayed fragility. The child eliminates the parent from their own mind so as not to suffer, until disappointment and a relationship between equals reopen thought. Reunion is a beginning, not a cure.

PART VI — INDUCED FALSE ACCUSATIONS

21. What False Accusations Are and How They Are Built

Nothing in what follows is meant to question the reality of domestic violence and child abuse, which exist and must always be recognized, prosecuted, and fought with every available instrument. This section refers exclusively to cases in which the accusation proves to have been constructed within a documented alienating dynamic. Distinguishing between well-founded and instrumental accusations is not an act of delegitimization: it is a necessity of justice for everyone involved, starting with the child.

Recognizing, understanding, and countering unfounded accusations in parental alienation contexts means protecting the child's right to a rigorous evaluation, grounded in verifiable evidentiary criteria and full respect for due process. It also means examining the psychological processes through which an account can form, consolidate, and crystallize: suggestion, identification, loyalty-dependent pressure, confusion between lived memory and narrated memory. When the justice system fails to distinguish between real trauma and the relational construction of trauma, the risk is not only procedural error. It is the fixing of a child's identity around a fracture, with effects that can extend well beyond the end of the proceeding. For this reason, addressing induced accusations does not mean denying violence: it means protecting truth, complexity, and the responsibility of those called upon to decide.

Defining in Order to Distinguish

To understand what happens in proceedings where grave accusations emerge, the phenomena must be named correctly. One of the main sources of error arises from the indiscriminate use of different terms treated as equivalent when they are not.

In the context of this book, a false accusation is an accusation that is wholly unfounded, devoid of objective corroboration, that does not correspond to events that actually occurred, and that is used as leverage within a relational conflict. Only when an accusation is entirely false can it be considered instrumental. Instrumentality concerns neither the intensity of the emotion nor the subjective conviction of the accuser, but the absence of a real event to which the accusation refers.

The term "false accusations" is often avoided in institutional settings, because it raises the fear of minimizing risk, of failing to protect the child, of "erring on the wrong side." This caution, however, can turn into conceptual blindness. Avoiding the term does not eliminate the risk: it only eliminates the possibility of thinking it, verifying it, and differentiating it.

To avoid confusion, four levels must be distinguished. A false accusation finds no support in any real fact; it may be sustained with emotional conviction, but it remains without factual foundation. An unfounded accusation arises from a subjective perception or a mistaken interpretation, without implying intent. An instrumental accusation is a false accusation used with a precise function: shifting the conflict from the relational plane to the moral plane, justifying the removal of the child, constructing a frame of dangerousness. A perceptual error concerns the subjective reading of ambiguous behavior, without a stable, repeated narrative construction. Confusing these levels produces enormous harm.

It is just as essential to distinguish among accusation, suspicion, and real risk. An accusation is a statement. A suspicion is a hypothesis. Real risk is a condition assessed on the basis of concrete, observable, verifiable indicators. When these three levels are conflated, the system stops evaluating and starts reacting.

The fact that a person has been accused does not mean they are dangerous. The fact that a child expresses fear does not mean abuse occurred. The fact that an account is emotionally coherent does not mean it is historically true.

When the system fails to define clear thresholds, it produces a double harm: it does not protect better, because it confuses real danger with hypothesized danger; and it creates harm, because it makes definitive what should be temporary and revisable decisions. In this vacuum of distinction, the false accusation finds fertile ground — not because it is "believed," but because it is no longer thought of as a hypothesis to be verified.

The False Accusation as a Defensive Instrument

To understand the phenomenon, the gaze must shift from blame to function, without thereby legitimizing the harm.

Defining the false accusation as a defensive instrument does not mean softening its gravity. It means recognizing that, in some contexts, the accusation is born not from the desire to recount a fact, but from the need to defend oneself emotionally, to preserve an internal equilibrium, or to avoid a confrontation experienced as intolerable.

One of the main engines is the protection of self-image. In highly conflictual separations, admitting the end of a bond or the complexity of one's own choices can be unbearable. The accusation offers a powerful way out: if the other becomes dangerous, the separation is no longer a choice but a moral necessity. The self-image is preserved through a narrative reorganization: I did not push the other parent away — I protected.

The false accusation also works as avoidance of relational responsibility. On the relational plane there are gray zones, ambivalences, shared responsibilities, mutual failures. On the accusatory plane there are only two positions: the one who protects and the one who is dangerous. This shift produces an immediate effect: the accuser is no longer called to examine themselves, their actions, their rigidities. The conflict is frozen, not resolved. And what goes unprocessed tends to harden.

The shift onto the moral and criminal plane is a further passage. As long as the conflict remains relational, it requires discussion, mediation, compromise. Once it becomes moral, it no longer requires dialogue: it requires taking sides. The accused parent is no longer an interlocutor to negotiate with, but someone to be defended against. The language changes, the roles polarize, every attempt at explanation is reinterpreted as further proof of guilt. The court system is sought not as a space of clarification, but as an instrument of definitive legitimation of a narrative already built.

At the base operates a simple, powerful logic: if I accuse, I save myself — from confrontation, from doubt, from the risk of losing control of the narrative, from the possibility that the child maintains a bond with the other parent. This logic is not always conscious. Often it structures itself progressively, through micro-choices that over time become a coherent strategy. Once underway, the accusatory logic tends to reinforce itself: any step back would call into question not only the accusation, but the entire identity construction organized around it.

When the false accusation is used as a defensive instrument, it tends to evolve through escalation: accusations that were initially vague or circumscribed become, over time, graver, more detailed, more extensive. Not because new facts emerge, but because the narrative needs to strengthen itself to maintain its credibility and its function. Every verification that produces no corroboration leads not to reconsideration, but to a stronger reformulation of the accusation. The problem is no longer the truth of the facts, but the durability of the narrative.

One of the most devastating effects is the freezing of dialogue. When the accusation becomes the pivot of the relationship, every attempt at communication is read as defense, manipulation, minimization. Dialogue is no longer possible, because it would presuppose the possibility of doubt. And doubt, in a defensive narrative, is experienced as threat.

The accused parent finds themselves in a paradoxical position: anything they say can be used against them, and any silence can be interpreted as confirmation. Explaining the defensive function of the false accusation does not mean justifying it. It means recognizing that the harm produced is not born from nothing, but from a weave of fragilities, rigidities, and unprocessed dynamics. Only by recognizing this function is it possible to interrupt the escalation, protect the child, and prevent the system from being used as an amplifier of the conflict.

The Narrative Construction of the Accusation

The false accusation never arises as an isolated event. It is built through a progressive narrative process. Its strength lies not in its contents but in the structure that holds them together.

The first step is the selection of facts: neutral or ambiguous behaviors are isolated from context and reread as signals. Whatever does not fit the narrative is ignored or expunged. Over time, the selection becomes a stable lens.

Next comes retrospective reformulation: past events are reread in light of the new narrative, taking on meanings they did not have. A gesture becomes a signal; a conflict becomes proof. The reformulation produces an effect of inevitability: "it was all there — we just hadn't noticed."

The use of emotionally loaded words — abuse, violence, manipulation, danger, trauma — does not simply describe a reality: it constructs one. It narrows the space for doubt and triggers intense emotional responses. The improper use of clinical vocabulary lends authority and an impression of competence, making the narrative more credible in the absence of corroboration. The use of legal terms as moral labels forecloses revision: the accused parent is no longer someone who did something, but someone who is something — dangerous, abusive, unfit.

One of the most powerful mechanisms is the illusory truth effect of repetition (Hasher et al., 1977): a statement repeated over time tends to be perceived as true, regardless of evidence. Repetition creates familiarity, and familiarity is confused with reliability. When the same narrative is repeated by the accusing parent, taken up by the child, and confirmed by the institutional context, it acquires a status of truth that is hard to dent. At that point, the problem is no longer proving the accusation false, but denting a reality already institutionalized.

In some cases, the narrative construction can be reinforced through demonstrative behaviors, such as simulating physical injuries or producing decontextualized images and videos. These elements do not in themselves constitute proof, but they have a strong emotional and symbolic impact: they make the narrative visible, tangible, hard to contest on the spot. The risk is that the image replaces evaluation and emotional urgency takes the place of critical analysis.

The accusatory narrative does not prevail because it is true, but because it is coherent, repeated, and sustained. Making this process visible does not mean denying real risk. It means preventing a narrative construction from being mistaken for an established fact. When the narrative process is recognized, thinking can reactivate. And only active thinking can truly protect.

In Brief. False, unfounded, instrumental: confusing these levels produces harm. The false accusation works as a defense — it preserves self-image, avoids relational responsibility, shifts the conflict onto the moral plane — and is built in stages: selection of facts, retrospective reformulation, emotionally loaded words, repetition that becomes truth.

22. The Involvement of the Children and False Memories

The Child as the Pivot of the Accusatory Narrative

In the construction of a false accusation, the involvement of the children is the most delicate and most damaging passage. The child is not the origin of the accusation: they are the point at which the accusation finds strength, continuity, and legitimation. The child enters this process not by choice, but by adaptation.

Once the accusatory narrative takes structure, the child becomes its fulcrum — not only as a subject "to be protected," but as a privileged witness, the bearer of a truth that appears incontestable precisely because it is spoken by a minor. The child progressively learns that some things must be said, others must not be named, that silence can be dangerous, that words can save.

One of the most powerful instruments is emotional blackmail, which rarely takes the form of explicit threat but operates through improper responsibilization: "only you can protect us," "only you can save us." The child is loaded with the role of guarantor of the adult's emotional safety. The constant use of "we" dissolves the boundary between adult and child. Dissent becomes betrayal; doubt becomes guilt.

The child's statements are not born as spontaneous assertions. They are the result of a process of progressive induction, made of repeated questions, suggested interpretations, selective confirmations. From the clinical standpoint, as Ceci and Bruck (1995) documented, this is not conscious lying but relational adaptation: the child speaks in order to stay safe within the bond.

Over time, the repetition of the account produces an overlap between what has been said and what has been lived. The account becomes memory. The memory becomes identity.

When the child comes to testify, their word is often the result of forced loyalty. The testimony can appear coherent, detailed, emotionally intense — characteristics mistaken for spontaneity when they are the effect of a deep adaptation. It is important to distinguish between the child who consciously lies (a rare case) and the child who can no longer distinguish historical truth from subjective truth (the norm in these contexts). The suffering they display is authentic. The event it refers to may not be.

False Memories

The scientific research agrees on a fundamental point: memory is not a faithful recording of facts but a reconstructive, dynamic, deeply influenceable process — above all in childhood (Loftus, 1997). Every memory is reconstructed each time it is recalled, integrating current emotions, later information, interpretations supplied by the environment, relational expectations.

In children, cognitive structures are still developing, and the capacity to distinguish among direct experience, imagination, and narrative is not yet consolidated. This makes the child particularly vulnerable to suggestion, especially when it comes from emotionally significant figures.

A memory can be induced without coercion. It is enough for a content to be suggested repeatedly, associated with strong emotions, confirmed by a trusted adult, and inserted into a coherent narrative frame. Suggestion operates all the more powerfully the subtler it is: apparently neutral questions, implicit interpretations, selective emotional confirmations can progressively steer the memory.

A false memory is not a lie: it is an experience lived as real. The child who recounts an event that never happened can do so with conviction, emotional coherence, and intensity, because for them that experience exists.

The child's suffering is real, even when the event is not.

Understanding this is fundamental to avoiding two opposite errors: accusing the child of lying, or sacralizing the account as irrefutable proof.

The nervous system does not distinguish between a trauma actually lived and a trauma remembered as real (van der Kolk, 2014). A false memory can produce real physiological effects — hyperarousal, hypervigilance, defensive responses, emotional dysregulation — configuring a form of psychological violence that produces authentic suffering in the absence of a real event.

When a false memory is internalized during development, it can organize the child's experience around a rigid representation: of self as victim, of the other parent as persecutor, of the world as dangerous. Over time it can foster chronic anxiety, difficulties with emotional regulation, dissociative states, cognitive rigidity, relational difficulty.

If the narrative is never questioned and the system confirms it over time, the false memory can consolidate and persist into adulthood. The child grows up with an identity story founded on an experience that never happened but was lived as real for years. Questioning it would mean questioning their own identity, their own choices, their own emotional history; this is why some adult children continue to maintain false accusations with absolute conviction. Not out of malice, but out of the psychological necessity of preserving internal coherence.

Addressing false memories does not serve to deny protection. It serves to strengthen it, because protection that fails to distinguish between historical reality and subjective reality risks producing irreversible harm. Only by recognizing how a memory was formed is it possible to truly protect the child without destroying the bond with the innocent parent.

A false accusation of abuse does not destroy only the unjustly accused parent: it can itself become a form of abuse of the child. The psychology of testimony and memory has shown that children, especially in emotionally charged and conflictual contexts, are highly suggestible. The international studies on false memories already cited in Chapter 3 (Loftus; Ceci & Bruck) have shown how an event that never occurred can be progressively internalized until it becomes subjectively real. European research, including the contributions of Professor Giuliana Mazzoni, has likewise clarified how childhood memory can be contaminated by suggestive questions, narrative repetition, and implicit pressure.

When a nonexistent traumatic history is attributed to a child and reinforced by inadequate questioning or an insistent family narrative, the psychological damage produced is not symbolic. The child ends up building their identity around an induced trauma, internalizing fear, disgust, and rejection. In clinical terms, the repeated imposition of a false abuse story constitutes a form of structural psychological violence. The damage is real, developmental, and deep, because it alters the sense of self, compromises the attachment bond, and affects emotional development.

To attribute to a child an abuse that never happened is to take from them the truth of their own history. When memory is manipulated, it is not just an account that is altered: it is identity. And altering a child's identity is, in itself, a form of abuse.

As Mazzoni, Scoboria, and Harvey (2010) observe, the inappropriate use of suggestive questions can produce inconsistent, senseless responses, damaging the witness's credibility and contributing to the formation of false memories in the most vulnerable subjects, including children. More specifically, Mazzoni and Rotriquenz (2012) showed that in cases of alleged sexual abuse, a child's memory is particularly susceptible to the influence of interview techniques: suggestive or repeated questions can alter the memory, incorporate external elements, or generate responses that do not reflect authentic experience.

The Devastating Effects and the Institutional Errors

Effects on the accused parent. When a false accusation takes structure, its effects do not stay confined to the courtroom. For the parent who suffers it, the initial impact is often an identity shock: it is not a behavior being questioned, but the entire person. The personal history, perceived until that moment as coherent, is suddenly rewritten from outside. Many parents describe a sense of unreality: "I don't recognize myself anymore; I no longer know how to defend myself."

Hypervigilance and constant alarm follow: every word or silence is experienced as potentially dangerous. The body stays on alert — insomnia, difficulty concentrating, muscle tension, chronic fatigue. The parent can no longer "switch off" the alarm system. Some react with emotional withdrawal, reducing emotional expression as a survival strategy; others with defensive reactivity, made of over-argumentation and a constant need to prove innocence. Both responses are adaptive in the short term but grinding over time.

One of the most painful aspects is learned helplessness, often accompanied by deep loneliness. Many parents feel isolated, disbelieved, avoided. It must be repeated: if you feel destroyed, it is not weakness. It is an understandable reaction to prolonged relational and institutional violence.

Effects on the children. The child caught up in a false accusation lives in a condition of chronic emotional tension. Forced loyalty pushes them to choose even when no one asks: every positive emotion toward the accused parent becomes betrayal; every doubt about the dominant narrative generates anxiety. This internal conflict consumes resources that should be devoted to growth, play, discovery.

Many children show diffuse anguish, irritability, withdrawal, over-adaptation — signals sometimes interpreted as proof of an original trauma, without considering that they may be a consequence of the accusatory context itself.

When the situation drags on, the risk is silent developmental damage: difficulty tolerating ambivalence, dichotomous thinking, low trust in relationships, difficulty integrating complex experiences. The child learns that the world is divided into good and bad, and that safety depends on adhering to a single narrative.

When Protection Becomes Harm

In proceedings involving false accusations, one of the most critical knots concerns how the institutional system interprets, manages, and crystallizes the accusation. Institutional errors almost never arise from bad faith. They arise from automatisms, from unexamined fears, from protocols applied without a real reading of the context.

One of the most recurrent errors is the conflation of accusation and truth: believing the accusation without verifying it. Real protection is born not from the act of believing, but from the act of verifying. Without verification, the accusation becomes an acquired fact, and every subsequent evaluation is steered in a circular way.

Caution, when it turns into a suspension of thought, becomes dangerous: the fear of being wrong leads to freezing relationships and cutting off contact with measures that, conceived as provisional, become structurally definitive.

The precautionary principle, when used in absolute terms and detached from contextual evaluation, produces the opposite effect: it treats every accusation as risk and every risk as certain danger. The failure to analyze narrative coherence — how the account formed, how it changed, who sustains it — produces superficial evaluations that mistake the account's coherence for historical truth.

The absence of alternative hypotheses prevents a genuinely clinical evaluation: the child's rejection is read only as the outcome of abuse, the suffering only as the consequence of an original trauma, the accused parent's silence only as guilt. A moralistic rather than clinical reading completes the picture: behavior is judged more than understood.

Recognizing institutional errors does not mean blaming individual professionals. It means taking collective responsibility for how protective criteria are applied. Only a system that keeps room for doubt, for verification, and for revision can truly protect.

When the system gives up critical thinking, protection stops being protection and becomes a form of indirect violence — silent, but deeply incisive.

A Message to the Parent

If you have been accused without facts to justify it: you are not invisible, you are not wrong, you are not dangerous by definition. The suffering you are living is not a personal fragility, but the response to a deep fracture, relational and institutional. Understanding what happened does not automatically give back what was lost. But it gives back meaning. And meaning is the first step toward not being definitively crushed by someone else's narrative.

In Brief. The child is not the origin of the accusation: they are the point at which the accusation finds strength. Memory is reconstructive, and a false memory is not a lie: it is an experience lived as real, which produces authentic suffering. Two errors to avoid: accusing the child of lying and sacralizing the account as proof.

23. Guidelines and Reading Grids

After working through the mechanisms of false accusations — defensive function, narrative construction, the involvement of the children, devastating effects, institutional errors — understanding must be turned into orientation.

Indicators of False Accusation

The indicators must not be read in isolation or used as labels. They take on meaning when they emerge coherently, repeatedly, and in context. Among the most relevant: the progressive, non-sudden construction of the accusation; the retrospective reformulation of facts; the constant use of emotionally loaded language; the absence of objective corroboration despite the repetition of the account; the active involvement of the child as spokesperson; narrative rigidity and the impossibility of integrating dissonant elements. It is their overall configuration that provides relevant indications.

Indicators of Real Risk

Distinguishing the false accusation from real risk is an act of protection, not of denial. Real risk presents recognizable characteristics: coherent, persistent behavioral signals; independent external corroboration; congruence among account, context, and clinical observations; the possibility of narrative variation without collapse of the structure; the absence of instrumentalization of the child in the conflict.

What a Correct Evaluation Should Do

A correct evaluation does not start from the search for a culprit, but from the understanding of the context. It requires time, room for doubt, and the capacity to hold contradictory elements together. In particular, it should distinguish among accusation, suspicion, and risk; analyze the genesis of the account; observe the relational dynamics as a whole; consider alternative hypotheses; provide for the possibility of revision. Rigidity is the enemy of protection. Authentic protection is dynamic, thinking, revisable.

The Clinical-Forensic Distinction Between False Accusations and Real Abuse

Real abuse is an event or series of events involving a concrete violation of the child's boundaries, characterized by indicators consistent over time and clinical findings compatible with traumatic experience. Protection in these cases is the priority and is non-negotiable.

False accusations are not defined by the absence of suffering in the child — the child often appears genuinely anguished. The fundamental difference lies not in the intensity of the emotion, but in the origin of the narrative and the relational context in which it takes structure.

As Warshak (2015) has shown, in alienation cases the false accusation can become a relational instrument to justify the exclusion of a parent. One discriminating criterion concerns the developmental coherence of the account. In real abuse, the narrative shows internal continuity, albeit with age-related variations. In false-accusation contexts, the account can stiffen, adapt to the adult's questions, present emotional incongruities, and show dependence on the relational context.

A further element is the child's position: in real abuse cases, the child shows internal conflict; in false-accusation cases, they can appear excessively aligned, devoid of ambivalence, judgmental, a champion of justice.

Note: the indicators listed here do not constitute diagnostic criteria and do not replace an individualized forensic evaluation; their use outside a complete clinical or forensic assessment is inappropriate and potentially harmful.

Recognizing a false accusation is not the same as minimizing abuse. The confusion produces a double harm: it exposes genuinely abused children to the risk of not being believed, and it forces other children to sustain inauthentic narratives.

A responsible evaluation requires analysis of the relational process, observation of the dynamic over time, and the capacity to tolerate complexity. Only by maintaining this distinction is it possible to truly protect the child — preserving both the safety of those who have suffered real violence and the psychological integrity of those who have been drawn into unfounded accusatory narratives.

A Message of Orientation

To those reading as professionals, this part asks for a responsibility: to keep thought alive even under pressure, to resist the temptation of immediate solutions, to accept complexity as an integral part of protection.

To those reading as parents: having tools does not eliminate the pain, but it restores orientation. Knowing that criteria, indicators, and possibilities of critical reading exist does not solve everything, but it prevents chaos from becoming destiny. To protect is to distinguish. To distinguish is to observe. To observe is to take on the responsibility of not simplifying.

In Brief. The indicators of false accusation and those of real risk must be read in configuration, never in isolation. A correct evaluation analyzes the genesis of the account, considers alternative hypotheses, and remains revisable: rigidity is the enemy of protection.

24. Real Cases

The cases that follow are drawn from American and European case law and court records. They are not meant to provide legal guidance, but to show how the themes addressed in this part find confirmation in the reality of actual proceedings.

Key Principles from the Case Law

Across jurisdictions, courts that have confronted induced accusations and alienating dynamics have converged on a set of working principles. They are worth stating plainly, because they translate the clinical material of this part into judicial method.

A criminal accusation against a parent — even one that leads to charges — does not by itself justify the automatic, indefinite suspension of parent-child contact: protective measures must be proportionate, grounded in concrete findings, and revisable. The accusation must not be allowed to function as proof.

When a child's rejection of a parent emerges in litigation, what must be examined is the formation process of the child's account — who shaped it, how it changed over time, what pressures surrounded it — not merely its content or the confidence with which it is delivered.

The dismissal or collapse of an abuse allegation does not automatically prove that the accusation was knowingly false: a finding of deliberate falsity requires proof both of the accused's innocence and of the accuser's awareness. The distinction between an unfounded accusation and a maliciously false one must be preserved in both directions.

Conversely, when the evidence shows that a parent deliberately induced a child to make false allegations, courts have treated this as serious, sanctionable conduct — relevant to custody, to damages, and in some systems to criminal liability — because it weaponizes the child against the other parent.

And finally: sustained denigration and obstruction of the other parent's relationship with the child, even without any criminal accusation, has been recognized by courts as a form of harm to the child that justifies modification of custody and compensatory remedies.

Five Cases from the United States and Europe

A) False allegations of abuse in custody litigation — AS v TH (False Allegations of Abuse), High Court (Family Division), England and Wales — [2016] EWHC 532 (Fam). In a dispute between parents, the mother made a series of accusations (including sexual ones) against the father; the judge concluded that the allegations were false and stressed the necessity of following rigorous guidance in evaluating accusations. An exemplary European case of judicially established falsity in children proceedings.

B) Multiplying allegations and the standard of proof in fact-finding — Re P (Sexual Abuse – Finding of Fact Hearing), Family Court, England and Wales — [2019] EWFC 27. A proceeding with a very large number of abuse allegations; the case is often cited for the rigor required in evaluating evidence and managing statements, especially when allegations proliferate and become a "narrative system."

C) Recovered-memory therapy and false memories: professional liability — Ramona v. Isabella, jury verdict 1994, Napa County, California. The father, Gary Ramona, obtained a favorable verdict against therapists and a health facility, on the claim that his daughter had developed false memories of abuse in therapy. A foundational case linking suggestion, memory reconstruction, subjective conviction, and relational harm.

D) Suggestive interviews and daycare accusations — McMartin Preschool Trial (1983–1990), California. One of the best-known daycare-abuse-panic prosecutions; the case is central to the debate on suggestive interviewing and institutional amplification. Outcome: acquittals and dismissals, no final conviction after years of proceedings. An emblematic example of the contamination of child testimony.

E) Mass miscarriage of justice — the Outreau case (trial 2004; appeal 2005, Paris Court of Appeal), France. An investigation and mass trial over an alleged abuse ring; on appeal, many convictions were overturned with numerous acquittals and the recognition of grave systemic failures. A European case showing how, in complex contexts, testimony and interpretation can produce detentions and convictions later disproven.

A European Case of Review: Recantation in Adulthood

One further European case deserves separate mention, because it closes the circle opened by the testimonies of Chapter 19. A father was convicted, with a final judgment, of sexually abusing his children. Years later, the children — by then adults — recanted, publicly stating that they had lied as minors under the influence and pressure of their mother. On review, the appellate court acquitted him. The case is a key reference for connecting memory, suggestion, divided loyalty, and the late reversibility of an induced narrative: the children's voices, once free of the alienating context, became the most reliable account of what had actually happened — and the proof of what had not.

Induced false accusations do not exist in a vacuum. They find fertile ground when the institutional system — courts, child protective services, custody evaluations — lacks the instruments to recognize them.

Part VII analyzes how the institutional context can become part of the problem, and how it can return to being part of the solution.

> **In Brief.** Cases from the United States and Europe converge on one point: what must be established is the mechanism by which the account was produced, not the label. Neither punitive automatisms nor the sacralization of the report: fact-finding, case by case.

PART VII — THE SYSTEM: SOCIAL CONTEXT, COURTS, AGENCIES, EVALUATIONS

A note on Part VII. Where data are cited, sources are indicated. Where systematic data are not available — as with the frequency of evaluative errors in custody evaluations, or the percentage of high-conflict proceedings with an alienating component — the text says so. The observations on the system's critical points describe documented structural problems, not a judgment of individual professionals.

25. When Those Who Should Protect Cannot See

The Social Context: School, Sports, the Outside World

What the reader crossed from the inside in Part II — the escalation, the evaluations, the taking of the bond seen through the parent's eyes — is observed here from the outside: no longer the lived experience, but the functioning of the system that produces it.

The context in which evaluations of parental alienation take place is that of a court system with structurally long timelines. In the United States, family law is state law, and there is no single national clock; but the practical reality is familiar to anyone who has litigated custody. A contested custody case routinely takes a year or more to reach trial; with evaluations, continuances, appeals, and modification proceedings, families can remain in litigation for years. Family court dockets are crowded, judicial turnover is high, and in many jurisdictions a custody case will be heard by more than one judge before it ends. In a parental alienation context, where time is the most critical clinical variable — because every month of interrupted contact consolidates the rejection and makes recovery of the bond harder — these timelines are not a neutral datum: they are part of the problem.

Alienation does not live only inside the family's walls. It often consolidates outside — in silence, in normalization, in the cautious attitude of those who observe without intervening. School, sports, religious education, friends, acquaintances: these environments are not neutral. They can become spaces of protection or places where the dynamic crystallizes. Very often, with no bad intentions, they become the second.

School is one of the first contexts where alienation becomes visible — and also one of the most inclined not to truly see it, because it tends to translate what it observes into manageable categories: "difficult divorce," "fragile child," "better not to get involved." This reading looks prudent, but it converts a potentially pathological dynamic into a normal variant of conflict. The alienated child at school appears polite, controlled, well-adjusted, with adult language and a narrative coherence that reassures. They are described as "mature," "very self-aware," "clear about what they want." But precisely this clarity makes the alienation invisible: a child who speaks well and seems decided is interpreted as free, not as conditioned. They learn early the phrases that close a conversation: "I don't see him by my own choice," "Being around her isn't good for me," "It's better this way." They show no ambivalence. They ask for no help. And since the account is linear, no one questions it. In sports, alienation passes even more unnoticed. Coaches and instructors look at behavior, discipline, performance. If the kid trains, follows the rules, causes no problems, the situation is read as functional. Many alienated children use the body as an emotional regulator: they take refuge in performance because it is measurable, requires no vulnerability, requires no words. For some it is a neutral space, for others a cage of perfectionism. Coaches rarely ask "how are you really doing?" — and when the child says they no longer see a parent, the implicit response is: "If they say it like that, it must be right." In religious or values-based educational settings, alienation takes a more complex form, because the moral register comes into play: right/wrong, guilt/responsibility. The child can deploy a moralized narrative — "he hurt me," "she's not a good person" — which reinforces the splitting, blocks all ambivalence, and makes the rejection "ethically correct." Once it becomes "right," it becomes untouchable. In the broader social context — friends, relatives, other children's parents — people tend to align with the more present version: the one heard most, seen most, that appears most coherent. The child appears polite, serene; they recount not an absence but a choice. And the more the adults accept that account as definitive truth, the more the dynamic consolidates. Most of these adults are not accomplices out of malice, but out of fear of being wrong. Many tell themselves: "I don't know the truth, so I shouldn't intervene." In these dynamics, however, silence is not neutral: it is a context that confirms. There is a crucial point: the alienated child, in most cases, does not seek help outside. Not because they would not need it, but because their internal configuration does not allow it. They present as someone who is "fine": coherent, determined, almost adult. But this solidity is often armor: it is not integration, it is holding. And every adult who fails to ask deep questions — out of fear, out of prudence, out of disorientation — involuntarily becomes an ally of the dynamic. The alienated child grows up in a world that does not ask, does not explore, does not name complexity. And so they learn to tell their story in simplified form, to defend a single version, to cut away part of their own history. Every time the account is accepted as definitive reality, the structure is reinforced. The price of normalization is that the child learns that feeling the pain is not worth it, that it is better not to complicate things, that the simple version works.

The Asymmetry of Perception Between the Two Parents

Almost always, one precise thing happens: the two parents are not perceived the same way. In the social fabric — school hallways, locker rooms, birthday parties, casual conversations — the family fracture is quickly narrated and classified. In the initial phase, the parent who appears abandoned tends to occupy the public stage of grief: they show themselves heartbroken, sometimes disheveled, repeating that they "wanted the family" and were betrayed. This posture elicits pathos and solidarity; the community, lacking tools to read relational complexity, adheres more easily to the emotionally more coherent version.

In parallel, the progressively excluded parent is portrayed as responsible for the rupture — accused of infidelity, domestic disengagement, lack of devotion — and ends up perceived as a cold or guilty figure.

All of this produces asymmetrical social images. It is not the facts that orient the judgment, but the representation in circulation. In school and sports contexts the dominant narrative consolidates quickly, and the public image precedes any critical analysis of events. One parent embodies the legitimate victim, the other the presumed cause of the harm. When reputation crystallizes before verification, complexity is replaced by an emotional simplification that orients alliances, judgments, and positions.

> **In Brief.** School, sports, and the social context are not neutral: by normalizing, they confirm. The alienated child appears mature and decided, and precisely this makes them invisible; the excluded parent is classified by the narrative in circulation, not by the facts. Silence is not neutral.

26. Interviewing the Child in Legal Proceedings

When the Child's Voice Is Not Free

In family proceedings one often hears: "Let's hear from the child — then we'll know the truth." In alienation cases this conviction can become a grave error. What we hear is not only the child's voice: it is often the voice of a relationship that has shaped them, that has taught them what may be said and what is too risky even to think.

A child can be subjectively sincere and, at the same time, psychologically conditioned. In a hearing, sincerity sounds like truth. Contrary to intuition, after age 12 the risk increases rather than decreases. What grows is the capacity to construct a convincing narrative — not necessarily a free one. The adolescent argues better, uses moral concepts, anticipates objections. Coherence is not a test of freedom: it is often a test of consolidation. As the international forensic-interview protocols show (Lamb et al., 2007), even when young people are honest, the quality of the information depends on how they are guided: closed questions increase contamination; neutral narrative invitations increase quality.

In the United States, this knowledge has been institutionalized in specific instruments. The NICHD Investigative Interview Protocol, developed by Michael Lamb and colleagues, structures the entire interview around free recall and open-ended prompts, precisely to minimize suggestion. Children's Advocacy Centers (CACs) — now numbering in the hundreds across the country — were created so that a child involved in an abuse investigation is interviewed once, by a trained forensic interviewer, in a child-friendly setting, on camera, instead of being questioned repeatedly by police, caseworkers, and attorneys. In custody litigation, judges in many states may interview the child in chambers (in camera), and the child's preference is one statutory factor — never the only one — in the best-interests analysis. These instruments embody the right insight: how a child is asked determines what a child says. But they are unevenly available, and in ordinary custody disputes — where no abuse allegation triggers a CAC referral — the child's statements often reach the court through far less protected channels: therapists' letters, guardian ad litem reports, the parties' own accounts.

The Preparation of the Child Before the Hearing

In alienation cases the preparation rarely takes the form of an explicit script. It is an emotional training that works through fear, guilt, loyalty, the need to protect.

Preparation by climate happens through repeated association between contact with the other parent and the distress of the parent the child depends on. The alienating parent's mood changes; they stiffen, go dark, sigh. The child learns an implicit rule: getting close to the other destabilizes. Preparation through victimhood turns the child into a "savior": "Only you understand me," "Only you know how things really are," "I can't make it without you." The message is: my equilibrium depends on you. At that moment the child is not thinking about the truth; they are thinking about not letting the adult they depend on collapse. Preparation through moral blackmail puts the child in an impossible position: it makes them feel that their word decides someone's survival. "If you don't tell everything, they'll take me away." "If you stay silent, we lose everything." The child internalizes that their word decides someone's life. The hearing stops being a moment of truth and becomes a test of loyalty.

Linguistic preparation supplies the child with formulas that block exploration: "It's my choice," "I don't feel safe," "I don't have to justify myself." They sound like sentences of autonomy; in alienating contexts they serve to close the conversation and prevent any deepening. Internal freedom is not measured by the perfect form of a sentence, but by what the sentence allows or prevents.

During and After the Hearing

In an alienation case the hearing is an emotionally charged moment, even when the child does not show it. The fear of the relational consequence: the child does not fear the judge; they fear the alienating parent's gaze on the way home, the reaction, the chill, the guilt. The need for coherence: when a narrative has been repeated and reinforced for a long time, questioning it would open devastating questions — "then maybe it isn't true?", "then maybe I judged wrongly?" — too heavy to bear. Adultification: the child recounts not emotions but reasons. They do not say "I miss him," "I'm confused"; they say "I've decided," "it's better this way." When explanation replaces emotion, the mind is protecting something too painful. After the hearing, the child's word is experienced as a definitive act. Once verbalized and formalized, the child feels bound by it. In the alienating context they receive powerful reinforcements: "You were so brave," "You saved us," "You told the truth." Or an anxious debriefing: "Did you say everything?", "Did you explain it right?" The narrative stiffens further, because now it is no longer only inside — it is also "out there," and it feels irreversible.

The Hearing as a Fragile Indicator

In suspected alienation cases, the child interview cannot be interpreted as self-sufficient proof of autonomy, cannot be read outside the relational context, and risks reflecting above all the stabilization of a narrative script. The child is not necessarily saying "what is false" intentionally: what they say may have been selected, reinforced, and consolidated until it became their subjective truth. The clinically sound formulation: in alienation, the child interview is a delicate instrument that requires specific competence and must be placed within a multilevel evaluation (Warshak, 2015). Taken as the only or main decisional indicator, it may measure the degree of conditioning and loyalty more than a genuinely autonomous choice.

A child should never find themselves thinking: "If I get a word wrong, I lose someone." When that happens, we are not listening to a choice. We are listening to a survival strategy.

> **In Brief.** A child can be sincerely convinced and psychologically conditioned: coherence is not a test of freedom. Preparation for the hearing works through climate, victimhood, moral blackmail, and formulas that close exploration. The interview is a right and a delicate instrument: never self-sufficient proof.

27. The Court and the Custody Evaluation

When Deciding Becomes Excluding

The court is where families arrive when they can no longer find equilibrium on their own. It is the place of decision. And in alienation cases it is also the place where errors can become structural — not through incompetence, but because the structure of the proceeding is designed for linear conflicts. Alienation is a layered relational process that produces an apparent reality very different from the psychological reality. The first problem is time. The court needs to decide: it has deadlines, caseloads, emergencies. Alienation needs to be understood, and understanding takes time. When the pressure to decide exceeds the capacity to analyze, decisions crystallize the existing situation. A child who rejects a parent is often left in the situation they are in. But not deciding is already a decision — and in most cases, it confirms and reinforces the alienating dynamic. For a six-year-old, six months of absence is a developmental era. For an adolescent, a year without the excluded parent can mean the definitive loss of a relationship. The court's time and the time of relationships are not the same time. The second problem is the seduction of the expressed wish. If a child says "I don't want to see my father" or "I don't want to see my mother," the system tends to hear that sentence as the end point. In alienation cases, it is often the end point of a process — not the expression of a free choice. The court needs clear decisions. But a child who rejects a parent is not signing a declaration of intent; they are responding to a system of pressures that has reorganized their emotional world. As Chapter 3 explained, a child's mind is not a notarized document: it is a relational survival system, in which loyalty to the parent they live with becomes the condition for feeling safe. The third problem is the accused parent's paradox. If they try to explain, they appear combative. If they stay silent, they appear indifferent. If they persist, they appear obsessive. If they withdraw, they appear unfit. Whatever they do can be read against them. Once the interpretive frame has been set, every behavior is filtered through it. A parent who cries in the courtroom is read as emotionally unstable. A parent who stays composed is read as detached. A parent who brings documentation is read as litigious. There is a specific pain many parents describe: the moment they realize the system is not listening to them. Not because anyone decided not to, but because the mental template has already been set. The questions are not seeking complexity; they are seeking confirmation.

Family justice should be the place where frames are interrogated, not confirmed. The place where someone asks: why is this parent suffering so much? What produced this situation? Who has an interest in maintaining the exclusion? When these questions are not asked, the proceeding becomes the ratification of a process already underway. When they are truly asked, they change everything.

When a temporary order suspends contact, it can last months or years. The child adapts to the absence, the narrative consolidates into certainty, the excluded parent wears down. An order suspending contact without setting a precise review date is not an act of prudence; it is an act of surrender. This is not protection. It is inertia disguised as caution.

The Custody Evaluation

The custody evaluation is the instrument through which the court entrusts an expert with the assessment of the family dynamics. In theory, it should guarantee the judge a competent, impartial reading of the situation. In practice, the quality of these evaluations varies enormously, and in parental alienation cases the errors can be especially grave. The assessment of parenting in a custody evaluation is a high-discretion operation. The American Psychological Association has issued professional guidelines for child custody evaluations in family law proceedings, and the Association of Family and Conciliation Courts (AFCC) has published model standards of practice; both insist on multiple methods, multiple sources, and transparency of methodology. But guidelines are not mandates: the choice of evaluative methodology largely remains with the individual evaluator, requirements for training and credentials vary from state to state, and the rigor of actual practice is uneven. Alongside the evaluator, other figures populate American custody litigation: the guardian ad litem (GAL) or, in some states, the attorney for the child, appointed to represent the child's interests; and the parenting coordinator, appointed in some high-conflict cases to manage day-to-day disputes after a parenting order. Each of these figures can be a safeguard — and each, without specific competence in alienating dynamics, can become another channel through which a constructed narrative is institutionalized.

There is also a properly evidentiary gate: under the Daubert standard (and, in a minority of states, the older Frye standard), expert testimony must rest on reliable methodology. This cuts both ways, and rightly so. Courts have excluded testimony presenting "parental alienation syndrome" as a validated diagnosis — and the same scrutiny obliges every expert, on any side, to ground their opinions in documented conduct and accepted method rather than labels. The methodological position of this book and the logic of Daubert converge: what belongs in court is observable behavior, its history, and its effects — not a name.

The first problem is training. Not all evaluators have specific preparation on alienation. Many apply models designed for ordinary conflicts to dynamics that are anything but ordinary. When the reading grid is inadequate, what is observed will very likely be misunderstood. The most frequent error is the static evaluation: the child is observed at a given moment, what they say is collected, what is visible is described.

But alienation is not a state; it is a process. An alienated child observed in a single session can appear serene, coherent, even happy. None of this says anything about the freedom of that position. Without a historical reading — how the rejection formed, when it began, how it evolved, what pressures acted on it — the evaluation confuses the result of the process with the reality of the child. As Warshak (2010) observes, the confusion between narrative coherence and historical truth is one of the ten most common errors in judicial evaluations of alienation.

To this is added the problem of time. A custody evaluation takes months to complete; in many cases it exceeds a year. In an ordinary conflict, the duration may be a procedural inconvenience. In alienation, time is a structural factor: it works in favor of the alienating parent.

While the evaluation is underway, the manipulation continues, the rejection takes root, the child adapts to the new relational configuration until they internalize it as their own. Every month that passes without intervention is a month in which the dynamic consolidates and becomes harder to reverse. The evaluator who files a report after a year is assessing a picture that has worsened in the meantime — and describes it as if it had always been that way. The absence of instruments allowing a rapid, targeted assessment in the early stages of the proceeding is one of the system's gravest gaps.

The evaluator is exposed to the same risk as every adult involved: allying with the more stable narrative. The alienating parent presents as cooperative and reasonable; the targeted parent can appear agitated, insistent — not because that is who they are, but because the situation has consumed them.

The perfect alignment between alienating parent and child is not a sign of health: it is often the clearest sign of the problem. But without specific competence, it gets described as a "harmonious" relationship.

The international forensic-psychology literature amply documents the incidence of cognitive bias in expert evaluations — from confirmation bias to the tendency to give excessive weight to the child's expressed wishes without assessing their authenticity.

In this context, the risk of evaluative error is double: the evaluator may fail to recognize an alienating dynamic in progress, or may attribute to alienation a rejection that has other causes. Both errors have grave consequences for the child.

A particularly critical knot is the child interview. The manipulated child does not present as a victim: they present as a witness. They speak with confidence, argue their rejection, supply reasons that appear reasoned and coherent. But that coherence is not the fruit of autonomous processing; it is the product of the programming they have undergone.

The words they use are not their own: they are the alienating parent's words, filtered through the child's voice. The evaluator who interviews an alienated child without tools to decode this dynamic takes as authentic a position that is induced, and transcribes it in the report as the expression of the child's wishes. It is one of the gravest and most frequent errors: transforming successful manipulation into proof of freedom.

The child is not choosing; they are executing. But their rejection, the moment it is accepted without critical analysis, becomes the foundation of the judicial decision. As if the coherence of the account guaranteed its truthfulness — when exactly the opposite is true: the more compact, structured, and ambivalence-free the child's account, the more reasonable it is to suspect it is not really theirs.

A child who speaks with nuances, contradictions, hesitations is a child who is processing. A child who speaks like an adult, without a margin of doubt, is a child who is repeating.

The evaluator's report carries enormous weight: it becomes the document on which the judge grounds the decision. If it contains reading errors, superficial interpretations, or omissions, those errors crystallize.

Challenging a custody evaluation is possible but extremely difficult: it requires time, financial resources, and the ability to find competent rebuttal experts. And in the meantime, the order based on that evaluation produces concrete effects on the life of the child and the excluded parent.

Many targeted parents describe reading the evaluation as one of the most devastating moments: seeing their own reality described in words that do not recognize it, their pain translated into "personality traits," their child described as free when they know the child is not.

There are no systematic studies measuring the frequency of these errors in American family proceedings — which makes the adoption of standardized protocols all the more urgent. Professional organizations have repeatedly called for structural reform of the evaluation system: more rigorous selection criteria, mandatory and continuing training, and quality-review mechanisms for filed reports.

This is why evaluator training on alienation should be a requirement, not an option. Specific competence is not a luxury: it is a necessity. Without it, the evaluation risks producing a document that is formally impeccable and substantively blind.

In Brief. The court's time is not the child's time, and the expressed wish seduces the decision-maker. The accused parent is in a paradox: whatever they do confirms the frame. And a custody evaluation without a historical reading photographs the result of the process and mistakes it for the child's reality.

28. Child Protective Services and Secondary Victimization

When Protecting Becomes Freezing

Child Protective Services (CPS) is often the first point of contact between a family and the institutional system. Its caseworkers operate under constant pressure: excessive caseloads, insufficient resources, enormous responsibility, fear of being wrong. This produces a predictable consequence: the tendency to manage rather than transform, to contain the conflict rather than understand it, to protect the child from the visible pain rather than from the invisible process that is harming them.

Caseworkers are not the targeted parent's enemies; they are often competent people working with insufficient tools. Alongside them, in many jurisdictions, stand CASA volunteers — Court Appointed Special Advocates — who give the child a dedicated voice in dependency proceedings. But the mechanisms through which even good will can become part of the problem must be named. The central question is: are we protecting the child from the symptom, or from the process that produces it?

A child who rejects a parent appears to suffer when "forced" to see them. The system's reaction is to reduce that suffering: suspend the visits, slow down, wait until "the child is ready." But the suffering is not caused by contact with the rejected parent; it is caused by the loyalty conflict that the contact activates. The child does not suffer because they see that parent. They suffer because seeing them throws into crisis the narrative they adhered to in order to feel safe. Suspending contact does not resolve the conflict: it freezes it. The child stops suffering visibly — and progressively loses the bond.

When the agencies mistake symptom reduction for problem resolution, they involuntarily become part of the exclusion mechanism. It is like giving a painkiller to a patient with an open fracture and concluding that, since they are no longer screaming, they are healing.

The agencies tend to interact more frequently with the custodial parent — often the alienating parent. This greater presence creates a relational advantage and a risk of unconscious alliance: the one seen more often is perceived as more cooperative. The targeted parent appears destabilizing: the one who asks, protests, will not resign themselves. It is the same mechanism that operates in the social context, but when it operates inside the agencies, the consequences are institutional.

Time is a critical aspect. The agencies operate on timelines incompatible with the child's developmental needs. Supervised visits get postponed, quarterly reviews become semiannual, team meetings slip, calendars stretch out awaiting an update no one requests. For a child, every week without contact is a week in which the bond weakens and the alienating narrative grows more solid. Slowness is never neutral: in alienation cases it is a form of decision — the decision to let the dynamic consolidate.

Many targeted parents recount realizing that the system was not working alongside them — not out of hostility, but out of immobility. And immobility, when a child is losing a parent, is one of the most silent forms of institutional abandonment.

All of this produces an experience many targeted parents know intimately but rarely find named: secondary victimization. The harm inflicted not by the family dynamic, but by the system that is supposed to remedy it.

The first form is not being believed. The parent recounts a complex, counterintuitive reality that is hard to prove. On the other side there is a child who speaks with apparent clarity and a serene parent. The implicit response — "maybe you should ask yourself why your child doesn't want to see you" — inverts the responsibility and turns the victim into the cause of the problem.

The second is being evaluated through the lens of the emergency. The targeted parent arrives before the system in a state of deep suffering. They arrive with trembling hands, with a folder of documents no one will read, after nights without sleep. They may be anxious, agitated, emotionally fragile. The system, instead of reading that fragility as the consequence of a trauma, reads it as a personality trait. The anxiety becomes instability. The persistence becomes rigidity. The pain becomes unfitness. The harm suffered is converted into evidence against them — as if, faced with a person bearing the marks of what they have endured, the system, instead of asking who wounded them, asked them to justify their scars.

The third is institutional loneliness. Not the absence of people, but the absence of recognition. When the system does not recognize what is happening, the parent loses not only the child — they lose the possibility of being understood.

There is a moment when many stop trying: not because the pain has passed, but because talking about it produces more suffering than silence. They withdraw. They stop explaining. They stop hoping anyone will understand.

This withdrawal is not healing. It is surrender. And the system, seeing the parent "calmer," may convince itself the situation has resolved. In reality it has only consolidated.

If you recognize yourself in these words, know this: your suffering is not excessive, not disproportionate. It is the understandable response of a person subjected to a prolonged, silent injustice. The fact that the system does not recognize it does not make it less real.

How the System Should Work

A system that truly protects does not react: it evaluates. It does not conflate accusation with risk; it does not confuse the child's rejection with an autonomous choice. When a child rejects a parent, the first question should not be "what does the child want?" but "how did we get here?"

When a parent is accused, the first question should not be "is it true?" but "what is the relational context in which this accusation arose?" Protection that does not distinguish between spontaneous and induced rejection, between well-founded and instrumental accusation, between free choice and defensive adaptation, is not protection — it is an automatism that can strike anyone. But distinguishing requires tools that today, in most cases, are not there.

Specific training on parental alienation is not optional. Judges, evaluators, caseworkers who operate in family proceedings should have deep knowledge of alienating dynamics, induction mechanisms, and the cognitive traps the process produces.

Without training, even the most competent professional risks confusing the result of conditioning with the expression of freedom, narrative coherence with reliability, silence with resolution (Fidler & Bala, 2010). Training does not mean taking sides. It does not mean deciding in advance that every rejection is alienation, nor that every parent who alleges manipulation is right. It means acquiring the tools to read what otherwise stays invisible — to distinguish, precisely, where without competence one can only guess. A trained professional is not a partisan professional: they are a professional less likely to be wrong.

Then there is time. And time, as we have seen, is not neutral. The previous chapters showed what happens when the system stops: the bond deteriorates, the narrative consolidates, the return becomes harder. The question now is what to do. Concretely, every order suspending contact should carry a short, binding review deadline — not a generic three months, but a date, a calendared hearing, a verification duty that does not depend on a party's prompting. Custody evaluations should be completed on timelines compatible with the child's needs, not with bureaucratic rhythms: if a child is six and the evaluation takes eighteen months, the system is evaluating a child who has meanwhile become someone else. The agencies should have active monitoring protocols — close-interval reviews, weekly calendared visits in acute phases, periodic reports that compel an accounting of what is observed. Not passive waiting. Not the silence the system mistakes for stability.

Time is the ally of alienation when the system stands still, and the ally of protection when the system moves with awareness.

Hearing the child is a right and a necessity. But hearing does not mean sacralizing. Competent listening asks: is this voice free? Was this account constructed? Is this coherence a sign of processing or of defensive consolidation? Treating the child's voice as self-sufficient proof loads them with an unbearable weight: being referee, witness, and judge of a conflict that does not belong to them. Truly listening to a child means not stopping at what they say, but asking what they cannot afford to say.

Then there is a problem that runs through the entire system and that no individual competence can solve alone: fragmentation. Court, evaluator, CPS, school often operate as separate compartments. The targeted parent tells their story to the attorney, then repeats it to the evaluator, then repeats it to the caseworker, then repeats it to the judge — and no one has the complete picture, because no one has read what the others have written. The teacher notices that the child no longer mentions one parent, but does not know whom to tell. The agency writes a report the evaluator does not read. The evaluator files a report the agency does not integrate into its work. The judge decides on the basis of documents that photograph different moments without anyone having put them in sequence.

A system that protects provides for coordination: interagency case conferences that are not bureaucratic rituals but places where information converges; shared protocols guaranteeing every professional access to the complete history of the case, not just the fragment that concerns them.

A mature system, finally, knows how to recognize its own errors. It provides for review mechanisms. It does not turn its decisions into irreversible truths. The dignity of a justice system is not measured by its infallibility. It is measured by its capacity to repair. And repairing, in alienation cases, means acting before time makes irreversible what could still be recovered. Some of these indications have already found a first legislative response: the next chapter examines it.

To the parent reading these pages after months or years of battles: your experience is real. The pain you feel is the consequence of a process that has a name and that can be understood. You are not the problem, even when the system seems to say otherwise. Your persistence is not pathology: it is love that does not give up.

To the professionals: your competence is necessary. But competence, without awareness of alienating dynamics, risks becoming a blind instrument. Getting trained is an act of responsibility toward every child who passes through your office.

To those who work in the court system: deciding without understanding the process that produced what you observe is not justice. It is administration of the surface. And the surface, in alienation cases, lies — because it was built to lie.

> **In Brief.** Suspending contact to calm the symptom freezes the process: it is not protection, it is inertia. Secondary victimization has three faces: not being believed, being evaluated in the emergency, being left alone. A system that truly protects evaluates, coordinates, sets review deadlines, and knows how to repair its errors.

29. The American Legal Landscape: The Best Interests Standard, Kayden's Law, and the Child's Refusal

The Constitutional and Statutory Frame

American custody law rests on two pillars. The first is constitutional: the Supreme Court has long recognized that parents have a fundamental liberty interest in the care, custody, and control of their children (Troxel v. Granville, 530 U.S. 57, 2000). A parent-child relationship cannot be severed or curtailed casually; the state needs serious reasons, seriously established. The second pillar is statutory: in every state, custody and parenting time are governed by the best interests of the child standard. The statutes enumerate factors — the child's relationship with each parent, each parent's capacity to support the child's relationship with the other, the child's adjustment, any history of abuse, and, with age-appropriate weight, the child's own wishes. Two of these factors matter enormously for this book's subject. Most states expressly direct courts to consider each parent's willingness to foster the child's relationship with the other parent — the so-called friendly parent factor — which makes sustained obstruction and denigration legally relevant conduct, not just bad manners. And the child's preference is one factor among many, to be weighed in light of age and maturity — never a veto, for precisely the reasons Chapters 26 and 27 set out: an expressed wish can be the end point of a process rather than the expression of freedom.

The method this entire book has argued for — observable conduct, documented over time, from multiple sources — is not foreign to this frame. It is this frame. American courts do not need a diagnostic label to act on a parent who systematically obstructs contact, coaches a child, or builds a campaign of denigration; they need evidence of the conduct. And under the Daubert standard examined in Chapter 27, evidence of conduct is exactly what survives scrutiny, while testimony built on a contested syndrome label does not. The legal landscape, in other words, rewards the same discipline the clinical landscape requires: facts, chronology, convergence — not names.

The Child's Refusal Before the Court

When a child refuses contact with a parent, American courts face the same fork this book has described from the beginning. The refusal may be justified — a protective response to violence, abuse, neglect, frightening behavior. In those cases the system's answer is protection, and nothing in this chapter qualifies that priority. Or the refusal may be induced — fostered and reinforced by the other parent's conduct: systematic devaluation, obstruction of contact, interference with communication, recruitment of the child into the adult conflict, emotional manipulation, the construction of dysfunctional alliances.

The two configurations call for opposite responses, and confusing them in either direction harms a child. Treating an induced refusal as an autonomous choice abandons the child inside the dynamic; treating a protective refusal as alienation delivers the child to the danger they were fleeing. This is the double risk Chapter 2 named, and it is the fault line that runs through the entire American debate. The answer to both errors is the same: rigorous, early, individualized fact-finding into the causes of the refusal — before time converts the error, whichever it is, into something irreversible.

Courts that have handled these cases well have done what the clinical literature recommends: they have examined the history of the relationship before the rupture, the chronology of the refusal, the conduct of both parents, the formation process of the child's account, and the proportionality between the stated reasons and the totality of the rejection. Courts that have handled them badly have done what this Part has warned against: ratified the status quo, sacralized the child's statement, or — the symmetric failure — used an alienation claim as a shortcut to dismiss an abuse allegation that deserved investigation.

Kayden's Law and the New Generation of State Statutes

In 2022, Congress reauthorized the Violence Against Women Act and included in it a provision known as Kayden's Law — formally, the Keeping Children Safe From Family Violence Act. It is named for Kayden Mancuso, a seven-year-old Pennsylvania girl killed in 2018 by her father during court-ordered unsupervised visitation, after a custody proceeding in which warning signs had been discounted. Kayden's Law does not directly regulate state custody proceedings; it offers federal funding incentives to states that reform their custody laws along four lines: requiring courts to consider evidence of past abuse and to treat child safety as a threshold concern; restricting the use of "reunification camps" and other treatments that cut a child off from a parent they are attached to, particularly where the program lacks scientific support; ensuring that expert witnesses who testify on abuse and family dynamics have genuine, relevant expertise; and mandating ongoing training for judges and court personnel on domestic violence, child abuse, and trauma.

Several states have since enacted legislation adopting or adapting these standards: California with Piqui's Law (2023) — named for another murdered child — which added mandatory judicial training and restrictions on reunification programs; Colorado (2023), which limited court-ordered "reunification treatment" and tightened expert qualification requirements; Utah and Maryland (2024), which updated their custody statutes on judicial training, expert standards, and the criteria for ordering reunification interventions; Tennessee, which restricted court-ordered reunification programs lacking scientific support; and Pennsylvania itself, which passed its state version of Kayden's Law in 2024. Other states have bills in progress.

It must be said plainly, because intellectual honesty is the method of this book: Kayden's Law was born primarily from the child-safety movement's concern that courts were using alienation claims to override abuse evidence — the second of the two symmetric errors. Some of its advocates are deeply skeptical of parental alienation as a concept. And yet the statutes the movement produced converge, point by point, with what this book has argued from the opposite shore. Consider what these laws actually require: that courts ground decisions in documented conduct and competent evidence rather than labels; that experts be genuinely qualified; that judges be trained to recognize family violence and trauma — and training that teaches judges to read coercive control equips them to read coercive control in all its forms, including the psychological coercion of a child against a parent; and that children not be subjected to drastic, scientifically unsupported interventions that sever them from an attachment figure. Every one of those requirements protects the abused child and the alienated child alike, because both are betrayed by the same failures: superficial evaluation, unqualified experts, untrained judges, and decisions that mistake a label — any label — for a fact.

The restrictions on reunification camps deserve a specific word. This book has argued throughout that with a child in an alienated configuration, force hardens and pressure backfires (Chapter 17), and that the goal of intervention is to create conditions in which the child can freely recover a relationship — not to impose one (a principle that runs through the entire clinical literature, and that American and European courts share: emotional bonds cannot be coerced). A drastic, abrupt intervention that seizes a child from one parent and isolates them with the other is precisely the kind of pressure this book counsels against — whichever direction it points. The genuinely effective answer to alienation is not a mirror-image coercion arriving years too late; it is the early, graduated, supervised, accountable response described in Chapter 28 and translated into protocol in Part VIII: intervene in the first ninety days, preserve continuity while the facts are established, set binding review dates, and never let the passage of time make the decision by default.

Civil Society and the Figure of the Guarantor: The FLAGe Experience

The conviction that a child caught in a refusal dynamic needs a dedicated, independent voice — and needs it early — did not arise in legislatures. It was prepared, for years, by the work of family associations on both sides of the Atlantic. In Italy, the first national organization devoted specifically to this phenomenon was FLAGe — Figli Liberi dalla Alienazione Genitoriale, "Children Free from Parental Alienation" — a national volunteer association founded in Quartu Sant'Elena on May 15, 2014, and formally registered in 2018. Its founder and national president is the author of this book. The association brings together parents, grandparents, and family members excluded without justification from the lives of minor children and grandchildren.

Its bylaws fix its purposes: public awareness and official recognition of parental alienation as emotional and psychological abuse; the establishment of centers for receiving families and recovering the relationship between alienated child and targeted parent; and — the point of particular interest here — the institution, in every region, of a guarantor: a dedicated figure charged with the immediate recognition of parental alienation and ready to intervene.

Reread today, that 2014 provision anticipated a need that legislators on two continents would come to recognize a decade later: a child caught between adults at war needs a voice that is third, independent, competent — and fast. The American system distributes that function among several figures — the guardian ad litem, the attorney for the child, the CASA volunteer, the trained judge that Kayden's Law-style statutes envision. The names differ; the intuition is the same. Timely recognition is not an organizational detail. It is the very condition of protection.

Operational Implications

In light of this landscape, every situation of parental refusal should be crossed by four fundamental questions. What are the concrete causes of the refusal? Do objective elements exist that justify it? Are there behaviors obstructing the relationship with the other parent? What interventions can be activated promptly to protect the best interests of the child?

For professionals, the indications converge with those of Appendix A: document observable behaviors, not impressions; reconstruct the chronology of the refusal; analyze the relational process, not only the content of the account; distinguish between subjective conviction and psychological truth. For parents, the new generation of statutes offers something concrete: a child's refusal and obstructive conduct are no longer matters the court can observe from a distance. They are facts that demand findings — prompt, evidence-based, and revisable.

Conclusions

The American legal landscape is converging, from two opposite directions, on a single method. The constitutional protection of the parent-child bond, the best-interests factors on fostering the other parent's relationship, the Daubert discipline on expert evidence, and the Kayden's Law generation of statutes all point the same way: away from labels, toward conduct; away from automatisms, toward individualized fact-finding; away from drastic late interventions, toward early, trained, accountable response.

The goal is not the search for labels, but the concrete protection of the child's right to grow up inside family relationships that are healthy, safe, and respectful of their developmental needs. Understand before labeling, observe behavior before interpretations, protect the right to love freely: on this point the law, the case law, and the perspective of this book converge. A child's refusal of a parent is no longer a private fact the proceeding records after the damage is done. It is a signal that obliges the system to look. And to look immediately.

In Brief. Best interests, the friendly parent factor, Daubert, and the Kayden's Law generation of state statutes converge on one method: conduct, not labels; early fact-finding, not automatisms; trained judges and qualified experts, not drastic late interventions. The abused child and the alienated child are betrayed by the same failures — and protected by the same rigor.

PART VIII — OPERATIONAL TOOLS

30. Intervening Immediately: A Clinical-Legal Protocol for Suspected Parental Alienation

Parental alienation, when it manifests as a child's unjustified, persistent, rigidly structured rejection of one parent, is not an ordinary conflict to be "managed," but a developmental dynamic that requires prompt, technically oriented intervention.

The decisive variable is time: legal time tends to stretch; the child's psychic time, by contrast, rapidly consolidates identity narratives. Every postponement, every suspension of parenting time, every untargeted procedural step can reinforce the crystallization of the rejection.

The moment a parent, initiating a separation, reports that the other is obstructing or sabotaging the bond with the child, the intervention must proceed on two parallel planes: psychological and legal.

1. The Psychological Plane: Containing the Relational Pressure

The first objective is not to "clarify the conflict between the adults," but to assess the developmental risk to the child. One must distinguish among rejection that is reactive to concrete conduct, rejection induced by relational pressure, and identity-based rejection already crystallized.

What is needed is a rapid specialized assessment (not generic psychotherapy and not mediation), conducted by a professional with specific competence in high-intensity parental conflict and manipulative dynamics.

The immediate clinical objectives are: interrupting the psychological pressure on the child; avoiding the suspension of contact; restoring continuous, predictable parenting time; protecting the child from repeated questioning and demands to take sides.

The clinical principle is clear: the relationship is maintained through continuity. Interruption reinforces the narrative of rejection.

2. The Legal Plane: Timely Decision and a Structured Framework

In the American system, the instruments already exist: rigorous application of the parenting order and of the best-interests factors that protect the child's relationship with both parents; appointment of a custody evaluator with specific competence in relational-refusal dynamics; where appropriate, appointment of a guardian ad litem or attorney for the child; a detailed, verifiable parenting schedule; and effective monitoring of obstacles to parenting time, with enforcement when orders are violated.

What makes the difference is not the mere existence of the rule, but its timely, specialized application.

Where the rejection is unjustified and persistent, intervention should be rapid — within a few weeks — with orders that are clear, not generic. Family mediation, in such contexts, cannot be considered the primary instrument, since it presupposes reciprocity and cooperation, conditions often absent in alienating dynamics.

The objective is not to "balance the parties," but to reestablish the child's relational continuity and prevent the structuring of an identity fracture.

In Brief. Two parallel planes from day one: a rapid specialized assessment that protects the child from pressure while keeping contact alive, and a legal response that sets a clear, verifiable, enforced schedule. The principle on both planes is the same: continuity protects; interruption consolidates the rejection.

31. Clinical-Legal Quick Reference

Operational Protocol — The First 90 Days

This box condenses into an operational sequence the protocol set out in the previous chapter and is designed for quick consultation; it does not replace a full reading of Chapter 30.

Guiding principle: In the first 90 days the objective is not to establish who is right. The objective is to preserve relational continuity while the facts are established.

1 — Immediate alert. Critical clinical signals: sudden, absolute rejection; adult language in the child; absence of emotional ambivalence; a rigidly denigratory narrative. Two or more indicators present: immediate activation.

2 — Priority clinical response (within 30 days). Rapid specialized assessment. Maintenance of parenting time. Protection from pressure and repeated questioning. Structured relational-reactivation interventions. Clinical objective: prevent the crystallization of the rejection.

3 — Priority legal response (simultaneous). Urgent order on the parenting schedule. Appointment of a custody evaluator with specific competence in complex relational dynamics. Active monitoring of compliance. Immediate reporting of any sabotage. Legal objective: guarantee continuity and verifiability.

4 — Stabilization phase (30–90 days). Structured coordination among judge, evaluator, and clinician. Periodic verification of the effectiveness of the interventions. Prompt correction of any obstacles. Risk indicator: progressive reduction of contact = worsening of the picture.

Systemic errors to avoid: suspending contact "to calm the conflict"; automatically equating the situation with mutual conflict; postponing intervention while awaiting mediation; leaving the child in an autonomous decision-making position on matters beyond their age.

In Brief. Ninety days, one objective: preserve continuity while the facts are established. Alert on convergent signals, clinical response within thirty days, simultaneous legal response, coordinated stabilization — and never the four systemic errors, beginning with suspending contact to calm the symptom.

Concluding Chapter

This book was born with a simple objective: to offer a first orientation in a field that is complex, often confused, sometimes denied, other times oversimplified. It is not a point of arrival and does not claim to be. It is a first map. A tool for beginning to see, to distinguish, not to get lost.

It is also, before anything else, the book I wish I had found. When I found myself inside these dynamics, what was missing was not information, but the possibility of organizing it. Technical texts, studies, important contributions exist — but they are often fragmented, too specialized, or far from what actually happens in daily life. What was missing was a meeting point between what is studied and what is lived. This book was born exactly there.

I wrote it first in Italian, for the families of my country. Much of the structured literature on parental alienation is in English; having studied in the United States, I could reach it — but most of the people who called our association could not, and I watched confusion grow in that gap: internet searches, technicalities, partial information, no way to know what to look at or how to read it. This American edition closes a circle: it brings back to English-speaking readers — with the courts, the agencies, and the laws of the United States in its pages — a map that was first drawn from lived experience and then tested against the international research.

Many technical books exist, but few truly try to hold together what happens in the dynamics, what the parent lives, and what the child goes through, without reducing everything to labels or easy explanations. This book tries to do exactly that: to maintain complexity without making it inaccessible.

The indications contained here are instruments of observation: they acquire meaning only when read as a whole, in context and over time. Understanding does not mean simplifying, and protecting does not mean taking sides automatically — it means knowing how to distinguish.

This is a work born with a declaredly humble intent: to be useful. Useful for those who are inside these dynamics, for those trying to understand them, and for those whose role calls them to evaluate them. But above all useful for the children, because they are the ones who carry the greatest weight of what happens.

If these pages manage even just to offer a first orientation, to reduce confusion, to prevent dangerous simplifications, and to give back a minimum of meaning to those who feel lost, then they will have done their job. Not as a definitive answer, but as the beginning of a more aware way of seeing.

APPENDIX A — GUIDELINES FOR PROFESSIONALS, FAMILY MEMBERS, AND PRACTITIONERS

These guidelines do not constitute a binding protocol or official practice standards. They represent a frame of attention, useful for reading situations of parental refusal with greater prudence and competence.

For Professionals

1. Do not confuse refusal with alienation. 2. Always check for possible autonomous causes in the child. 3. Analyze the relational process, not only the content of the account. 4. Treat the chronology of events as a central element. 5. Pay attention to the child's merely apparent coherence. 6. Distinguish between subjective conviction and psychological truth. 7. Avoid premature labels and binary readings. 8. Document observable behaviors, not mere impressions.

For Family Members

1. Do not ask the child to choose. 2. Do not use the child as a confidant or ally. 3. Do not speak of the other parent in devaluing terms. 4. Do not interpret every refusal as definitive proof. 5. Protect the child's right to emotional complexity. 6. Recognize that the child can appear convinced without being truly free.

For School, Social Services, and Healthcare Personnel

1. Do not automatically assume the prevailing narrative is neutral. 2. Consider the relational context in which the child's voice takes shape. 3. Avoid unconscious alliances with the emotionally dominant party. 4. Flag the need for specialized evaluation when multiple, persistent indicators emerge. 5. Maintain a prudent, descriptive, non-ideological approach.

APPENDIX B — SYNOPTIC TABLE OF THE TWENTY DYNAMICS

The table that follows summarizes the twenty relational dynamics described in Chapter 4, for quick consultation. The rule established in that chapter applies: no dynamic, considered in isolation, is indicative; what matter are convergence, persistence over time, and the plurality of observation sources.

Dynamic 1 — Normalized everyday disparagement. How it shows itself: negative comments and allusions about the other parent, repeated and apparently harmless. Effect on the child: they stop trusting their own experience and look at the parent through someone else's eyes.

Dynamic 2 — The one-way narrative. How it shows itself: a single version of the family history, presented as absolute truth. Effect: understanding becomes dangerous; remembering becomes betrayal.

Dynamic 3 — Protection that actually isolates. How it shows itself: fear used as leverage ("with me you're safe; with the other you're not"). Effect: learned fear in the absence of real danger.

Dynamic 4 — Selective emotional withdrawal. How it shows itself: silences and coldness whenever the child mentions the other parent. Effect: they stop telling, then stop naming, then stop feeling.

Dynamic 5 — Using the child as emotional support. How it shows itself: the child becomes the adult's confidant and consoler ("I couldn't make it without you"). Effect: obligatory emotional loyalty; loving the other means hurting the one who depends on them.

Dynamic 6 — Blurring the boundary between the adult world and the child's world. How it shows itself: the child drawn into adult matters: lawsuits, money, grudges. Effect: hyper-responsibility and guilt; from child to witness, ally, judge.

Dynamic 7 — Turning the parent into a caricature. How it shows itself: the parent reduced to a label without complexity. Effect: the world divided into good and bad, and that split carried inside.

Dynamic 8 — Systematic obstruction of contact. How it shows itself: calls not put through, "forgotten" messages, postponed visits, endless last-minute hitches. Effect: the bond dies by absence, and the rejection appears to be the child's choice.

Dynamic 9 — Rewriting memory and the past. How it shows itself: positive memories denied, minimized, or reinterpreted. Effect: the child loses the continuity of their own history.

Dynamic 10 — Coerced loyalty. How it shows itself: loving both is not possible; every affection toward the other has a cost. Effect: they choose for emotional survival; longing becomes a dangerous secret.

Dynamic 11 — Language that does not fit the child's age. How it shows itself: adult labels ("manipulator," "narcissist") without concrete episodes. Effect: language becomes protection, not expression.

Dynamic 12 — The absence of emotional ambivalence. How it shows itself: one parent idealized, the other demonized, without nuance. Effect: they feel only the "permitted" emotions; the others get buried.

Dynamic 13 — Extending the refusal to the entire relational world. How it shows itself: grandparents, aunts and uncles, cousins, friends, places — erased. Effect: isolation from half of their world and their memories.

Dynamic 14 — Symbolic replacement of the parental role. How it shows itself: new figures encouraged to occupy the excluded parent's place. Effect: the need for the parent becomes unspeakable; the void remains.

Dynamic 15 — Minimizing or denying the excluded parent's pain. How it shows itself: the other's suffering mocked, justified, or rendered irrelevant. Effect: the child learns that feeling compassion is wrong.

Dynamic 16 — Systematic attribution of bad intentions. How it shows itself: every gesture of the other read as malicious. Effect: chronic distrust; kindness is no longer recognizable as genuine.

Dynamic 17 — The illusion of choice. How it shows itself: "you decide," in an emotional context already steered. Effect: the coercion becomes invisible and the responsibility falls on the child.

Dynamic 18 — Exclusive emotional dependence. How it shows itself: "only I truly understand you"; no other bond is safe. Effect: autonomy becomes betrayal.

Dynamic 19 — Denying time and the history of the relationship. How it shows itself: "you never liked being with him"; the rejection presented as an original truth. Effect: part of a life erased, a nameless void.

Dynamic 20 — The loss of the right to love freely. How it shows itself: no words are needed anymore: the child knows that loving that parent is not safe. Effect: the deepest loss, into which all the others flow.

GLOSSARY OF TECHNICAL TERMS

Absence of ambivalence. Emotional rigidity in which the child describes one parent as entirely good and the other as entirely bad, without nuance or contradiction.

Adaptive configuration. The relatively stable way a child organizes thoughts, emotions, and behaviors to adapt to a relational context perceived as threatening or non-negotiable.

Alienated child. A child who, within an alienating dynamic, develops rejection, hostility, or emotional distance toward one parent as the adaptive outcome of prolonged relational pressure.

Alienating behaviors. The set of observable conducts through which a parent negatively influences the child's perception of the other parent: devaluation, obstruction of contact, rewriting of the past, attribution of bad intentions, involvement of the child in the adult conflict.

Alienating parent. A parent who enacts, consciously or unconsciously, repeated behaviors aimed at devaluing, obstructing, or compromising the relationship between the child and the other parent.

Alignment. The child's siding with one of the two parents as an adaptive response to family conflict, not necessarily produced by systematic manipulation.

Attachment. The primary emotional bond the child develops with the caregiving figures on whom protection, safety, and emotional regulation depend.

Attachment figure. The adult perceived by the child as a secure base and primary emotional point of reference.

Best interests of the child. The governing standard in American custody law: the court decides custody and parenting time according to statutory factors centered on the child's welfare, including each parent's capacity to support the child's relationship with the other parent.

Burden of proof. The need, in evaluative and judicial settings, to document a given hypothesis with convergent elements, without treating it as certain in the absence of sufficient corroboration.

Child Protective Services (CPS). The state agency charged with receiving, screening, and investigating reports of child abuse and neglect, and with intervening to protect children at risk.

Child interview. The activity of gathering the child's voice, perceptions, and lived experience in proceedings that concern them, to be conducted with criteria appropriate to age and context.

Coerced loyalty. An intense form of loyalty conflict in which the child feels they must emotionally choose only one parent in order to maintain safety, belonging, or affection.

Continuum. An interpretive model in which a phenomenon is not absolutely present or absent, but falls along a gradient of intensity, complexity, and severity.

Convergent indicator. An observational element that acquires interpretive value when it appears together with other consistent data pointing in the same direction.

Critical thinking. The capacity to evaluate information, distinguish facts from interpretations, tolerate doubt, and modify one's convictions in light of new elements.

Custodial parent (primary residential parent). The parent with whom the child habitually resides, even where legal custody is shared.

Custody evaluation. A technical assessment ordered by the court and entrusted to a mental-health professional, serving as specialized support for the judicial decision on custody and parenting time.

Differential evaluation. The clinical and forensic procedure aimed at distinguishing among alternative hypotheses that could explain the child's refusal, avoiding diagnostic shortcuts.

Disorganized attachment. The attachment pattern, described by Main and Solomon, in which the child has no coherent strategy toward the caregiving figure, because the source of safety coincides with the source of fear. In alienating contexts it can constitute the matrix of the child's adaptive configurations.

Emotional dependence. The condition in which the child feels that the parent's psychological well-being depends on them, taking on an emotional responsibility incompatible with their developmental role.

Emotional regulation. The capacity to recognize, modulate, and integrate emotional states without being overwhelmed by them or having to deny them.

Guardian ad litem (GAL). A person appointed by the court to represent the child's best interests in litigation; in some states, an attorney for the child performs a parallel function.

Induced false accusations. Accusations or accusatory accounts that can emerge in a child as the outcome of psychological pressure, narrative repetition, suggestive questioning, or relational conditioning.

Induced refusal. A refusal that develops mainly as a consequence of psychological conditioning, relational pressure, or narrative manipulation exercised by the other parent.

Joint custody. The legal arrangement that assigns parental responsibility to both parents and requires sharing of major decisions concerning the child.

Language that does not fit the child's age. The child's use of expressions, clinical or legal categories, or moralizing labels incongruent with their developmental level and plausibly derived from adult language.

Loyalty conflict. The psychological condition in which the child perceives that loving, listening to, or spending time with one parent amounts to betraying the other.

Memory rewriting. The process through which memories and episodes of the past are reinterpreted, denied, or distorted to make them consistent with the present rejection.

Neurosequential model. The model of brain development (Perry) according to which the brain matures from the bottom up: the areas that regulate stress are structured before those of critical thinking. It explains why early relational experiences imprint on the bodily plane before the verbal one.

Normalized everyday disparagement. A form of indirect, repeated denigration of the other parent through phrases, tones, allusions, and comments that are apparently harmless but constant.

One-way narrative. A rigidly unilateral family version, offered to the child as the only possible truth, with no room for ambivalence, doubt, or complexity.

Parental alienation. A dysfunctional relational process in which a child comes to persistently reject an adequate, emotionally available parent because of systematic psychological influence exercised by the other parent.

Parentification. The reversal of relational roles in which the child is invested with emotional, psychological, or practical tasks that belong to the adult.

Parenting coordinator. A professional appointed in some high-conflict cases to manage day-to-day disputes over the implementation of a parenting order, with limited decision-making or recommendation authority.

Phenomenological. A term indicating a description centered on what is observed and manifested in experience, without automatically attributing diagnostic labels.

Prefrontal cortex. The brain region involved in impulse control, evaluation of information, planning, and critical integration of experience. Its maturation continues into early adulthood.

Prolonged traumatic stress. The condition of psychophysical wearing-down resulting from extended exposure to pain, helplessness, relational threat, or unprocessable loss.

Protective refusal. A refusal grounded in direct experiences of fear, neglect, abuse, maltreatment, or grave parental inadequacy. In these cases the refusal is a defensive response, not a manipulative outcome.

Psychodynamic configuration. The recurring arrangement of defenses, fears, needs, conflicts, and relational patterns observable in a person's functioning.

Psychosomatic symptoms. Bodily manifestations connected to psychological suffering, such as tension, pain, gastrointestinal disturbances, headaches, or persistent fatigue.

Reconstructive memory. The characteristic of memory by which recollections are not perfect reproductions of the past but can be modified by later narratives, suggestion, and relational context.

Refusal by the child. An expression of opposition, closure, or denial toward a parent. It does not automatically coincide with alienation and always requires differential evaluation.

Relational dehumanization. The process through which the excluded parent's pain, feelings, or dignity are denied, ridiculed, or rendered irrelevant.

Relational model. A theoretical frame that interprets a phenomenon not as an isolated individual trait, but as the outcome of repeated interactions among several subjects within a system.

Relational system. The set of relationships, roles, alliances, and shared meanings within which family life develops.

Reunification therapy. Any of various court-ordered interventions intended to restore a parent-child relationship. Programs that abruptly sever a child from a preferred parent, or lack scientific support, have been restricted by Kayden's Law-generation statutes; graduated, supervised, accountable interventions remain the sound alternative.

Right to both parents. The principle that the child has the right to maintain balanced, continuous relationships with both parents, absent concrete prejudicial circumstances.

Secondary victimization. The additional suffering produced by institutional, healthcare, school, or judicial responses that fail to correctly recognize the complexity of the situation or further expose the person to harm.

Selective emotional withdrawal. The withdrawal of warmth, availability, or approval by a parent when the child shows interest, affection, or openness toward the other parent.

Splitting. The psychological mechanism that rigidly separates positive and negative aspects of experience, preventing an integrated representation of attachment figures.

Suggestibility in children. The particular vulnerability of a child to assimilating as their own information, convictions, or memories introduced by significant or authoritative adults.

Targeted parent. The parent progressively rejected, excluded, or delegitimized in the relationship with the child, in the absence of a sufficient autonomous cause in the child to justify the rejection.

BIBLIOGRAPHY

Ainsworth, M. D. S., Blehar, M. C., Waters, E., & Wall, S. (1978). *Patterns of attachment: A psychological study of the Strange Situation.* Lawrence Erlbaum Associates.

American Psychiatric Association (2022). *Diagnostic and statistical manual of mental disorders* (5th ed., text revision; DSM-5-TR). American Psychiatric Publishing.

Asch, S. E. (1956). Studies of independence and conformity: I. A minority of one against a unanimous majority. *Psychological Monographs: General and Applied, 70*(9), 1–70.

Baker, A. J. L. (2007). *Adult children of parental alienation syndrome: Breaking the ties that bind.* W. W. Norton & Company.

Baker, A. J. L., & Darnall, D. (2006). Behaviors and strategies employed in parental alienation: A survey of parental experiences. *Journal of Divorce & Remarriage, 45*(1–2), 97–124.

Baker, A. J. L., & Fine, P. R. (2014). *Surviving parental alienation: A journey of hope and healing.* Rowman & Littlefield.

Baker, A. J. L., & Verrocchio, M. C. (2016). Exposure to parental alienation and subsequent anxiety and depression in Italian adults. *The American Journal of Family Therapy, 44*(5), 254–266.

Bala, N., Hunt, S., & McCarney, C. (2010). Parental alienation: Canadian court cases 1989–2008. *Family Court Review, 48*(1), 164–179.

Bernet, W., von Boch-Galhau, W., Baker, A. J. L., & Morrison, S. L. (2010). Parental alienation, DSM-V, and ICD-11. *The American Journal of Family Therapy, 38*(2), 76–187.

Bowlby, J. (1969). *Attachment and loss: Vol. 1. Attachment.* Basic Books.

Bowlby, J. (1973). *Attachment and loss: Vol. 2. Separation: Anxiety and anger.* Basic Books.

Bowlby, J. (1980). *Attachment and loss: Vol. 3. Loss: Sadness and depression.* Basic Books.

Ceci, S. J., & Bruck, M. (1995). *Jeopardy in the courtroom: A scientific analysis of children's testimony.* American Psychological Association.

Childress, C. A. (2015). *An attachment-based model of parental alienation: Foundations.* Oaksong Press.

Crittenden, P. M. (1995). Attachment and psychopathology. In S. Goldberg, R. Muir & J. Kerr (Eds.), *Attachment theory: Social, developmental, and clinical perspectives* (pp. 367–406). Analytic Press.

Erikson, E. H. (1968). *Identity: Youth and crisis.* Norton.

Fidler, B. J., & Bala, N. (2010). Children resisting postseparation contact with a parent: Concepts, controversies, and conundrums. *Family Court Review, 48*(1), 10–47.

Fidler, B. J., Bala, N., & Saini, M. A. (2013). *Children who resist postseparation parental contact: A differential approach for legal and mental health professionals.* Oxford University Press.

Fonagy, P., Gergely, G., Jurist, E. L., & Target, M. (2002). *Affect regulation, mentalization, and the development of the self.* Other Press.

Freeman, D. (2007). Suspicious minds: The psychology of persecutory delusions. *Clinical Psychology Review, 27*(4), 425–457.

Garber, B. D. (2020). Parental alienation and the dynamics of the enmeshed parent-child dyad: Adultification, parentification, and infantilization. *Family Court Review, 58*(2), 322–335.

Gunderson, J. G. (2001). *Borderline personality disorder: A clinical guide.* American Psychiatric Publishing.

Harman, J. J., Kruk, E., & Hines, D. A. (2018). Parental alienating behaviors: An unacknowledged form of family violence. *Psychological Bulletin, 144*(12), 1275–1299.

Harman, J. J., Leder-Elder, S., & Biringen, Z. (2019). Prevalence of adults who are the targets of parental alienating behaviors and their impact. *Children and Youth Services Review, 106,* Article 104471.

Harman, J. J., Lorandos, D., & Bernet, W. (2023). Gender and child custody outcomes across 16 years of published family court cases involving parental alienation. *Children and Youth Services Review, 153,* Article 107125.

Harman, J. J., & Matthewson, M. L. (2020). Parental alienating behaviors. In D. Lorandos & W. Bernet (Eds.), *Parental alienation: Science and law* (pp. 82–141). Charles C Thomas.

Harold, G. T., & Sellers, R. (2018). Annual research review: Interparental conflict and youth psychopathology: An evidence review and practice focused update. *Journal of Child Psychology and Psychiatry, 59*(4), 374–402.

Hasher, L., Goldstein, D., & Toppino, T. (1977). Frequency and the conference of referential validity. *Journal of Verbal Learning and Verbal Behavior, 16*(1), 107–112.

Johnston, J. R. (2003). Parental alignments and rejection: An empirical study of alienation in children of divorce. *Journal of the American Academy of Psychiatry and the Law, 31*(2), 158–170.

Johnston, J. R., Walters, M. G., & Olesen, N. W. (2005). Is it alienating parenting, role reversal or child abuse? A study of children's rejection of a parent in child custody disputes. *Journal of Emotional Abuse, 5*(4), 191–218.

Kashdan, T. B., & Rottenberg, J. (2010). Psychological flexibility as a fundamental aspect of health. *Clinical Psychology Review, 30*(7), 865–878.

Kelly, J. B., & Johnston, J. R. (2001). The alienated child: A reformulation of parental alienation syndrome. *Family Court Review, 39*(3), 249–266.

Kernberg, O. F. (1975). *Borderline conditions and pathological narcissism.* Jason Aronson.

Lamb, M. E., Orbach, Y., Hershkowitz, I., Esplin, P. W., & Horowitz, D. (2007). A structured forensic interview protocol improves the quality and informativeness of investigative interviews with children. *Child Abuse & Neglect, 31*(11–12), 1201–1231.

Lee-Maturana, S., Matthewson, M., & Dwan, C. (2019). Characteristics and experiences of targeted parents of parental alienation from their own perspective: A systematic literature review. *Australian Journal of Psychology, 72*(1), 83–91.

Loftus, E. F. (1997). Creating false memories. *Scientific American, 277*(3), 70–75.

Main, M., & Solomon, J. (1990). Procedures for identifying infants as disorganized/disoriented during the Ainsworth Strange Situation. In M. T. Greenberg, D. Cicchetti & E. M. Cummings (Eds.), *Attachment in the preschool years* (pp. 121–160). University of Chicago Press.

Mazzoni, G., Scoboria, A., & Harvey, L. (2010). Nonbelieved memories. *Psychological Science, 21*(9), 1334–1340.

Mazzoni, G., & Rotriquenz, E. (2012). *La testimonianza nei casi di abuso sessuale sui minori* [Testimony in cases of child sexual abuse]. Giuffrè. (In Italian.)

Meier, J. S. (2020). Mothers risk loss of custody in cases involving parental alienation and abuse allegations. *Domestic Violence Report, 25*(4), 69–70, 83–84.

Milgram, S. (1963). Behavioral study of obedience. *Journal of Abnormal and Social Psychology, 67*(4), 371–378.

Minuchin, S. (1974). *Families and family therapy.* Harvard University Press.

Perry, B. D. (2009). Examining child maltreatment through a neurodevelopmental lens: Clinical applications of the neurosequential model of therapeutics.*Journal of Loss and Trauma, 14*(4), 240–255.

Perry, B. D., & Szalavitz, M. (2017). *The boy who was raised as a dog: And other stories from a child psychiatrist's notebook* (3rd ed.). Basic Books.

Piaget, J. (1970). *Science of education and the psychology of the child.* Viking.

Pincus, A. L., & Lukowitsky, M. R. (2010). Pathological narcissism and narcissistic personality disorder. *Annual Review of Clinical Psychology, 6,* 421–446.

Portilla-Saavedra, D., Pinto-Cortez, C., & Moya-Vergara, R. (2023). Psychological distress in young Chilean adults exposed to parental alienating behaviors during childhood/adolescence. *European Journal of Investigation in Health, Psychology and Education, 13*(9), Article 123.

Poustie, C., Matthewson, M., & Balmer, S. (2018). The forgotten parent: The targeted parent perspective of parental alienation. *Journal of Family Issues, 39*(12), 3298–3323.

Saini, M., Johnston, J. R., Fidler, B. J., & Bala, N. (2016). Empirical studies of alienation. In L. Drozd, M. Saini & N. Olesen (Eds.), *Parenting plan evaluations: Applied research for the family court* (2nd ed., pp. 374–430). Oxford University Press.

Schore, A. N. (2003). *Affect dysregulation and disorders of the self.* W. W. Norton.

Siegel, D. J. (2020). *The developing mind: How relationships and the brain interact to shape who we are* (3rd ed.). Guilford Press.

Stark, E. (2007). *Coercive control: How men entrap women in personal life.* Oxford University Press.

Tavares, A., Crespo, C., & Ribeiro, M. T. (2021). What does it mean to be a targeted parent? Parents' experiences in the context of parental alienation. *Journal of Child and Family Studies, 30,* 1375–1390.

Vaillant, G. E. (1986). *Empirical studies of ego mechanisms of defense.* American Psychiatric Press.

Vaillant, G. E. (1992). *Ego mechanisms of defense: A guide for clinicians and researchers.* American Psychiatric Press.

van der Kolk, B. A. (2014). *The body keeps the score: Brain, mind, and body in the healing of trauma.* Viking.

Verhaar, S., Matthewson, M. L., & Bentley, C. (2022). The impact of parental alienating behaviours on the mental health of adults alienated in childhood. *Children, 9*(4), 475.

Warshak, R. A. (2010). *Divorce poison: How to protect your family from bad-mouthing and brainwashing* (rev. ed.). Harper Paperbacks.

Warshak, R. A. (2015). Ten parental alienation fallacies that compromise decisions in court and in therapy. *Professional Psychology: Research and Practice, 46*(4), 235–249.

www.ingramcontent.com/pod-product-compliance
Lightning Source LLC
LaVergne TN
LVHW022027051126
851858LV00004B/70
* 9 7 9 1 2 9 8 6 5 1 6 0 9 *